COMIC BOOKS

COMIC
BOOKS

Comic Books

EXAMINING POP CULTURE

DAVID M. HAUGEN, Book Editor

Bruce Glassman, Vice President
Bonnie Szumski, Publisher
Helen Cothran, Managing Editor

GREENHAVEN PRESS
An imprint of Thomson Gale, a part of The Thomson Corporation

THOMSON
★
™
GALE

Detroit • New York • San Francisco • San Diego • New Haven, Conn.
Waterville, Maine • London • Munich

Cover credit: © Hulton Archive by Getty Images. In 1952 two boys lean against a wall engrossed in one of the times' most popular forms of entertainment, reading comic books featuring their favorite superheroes.

LIBRARY OF CONGRESS CATALOGING-IN-PUBLICATION DATA

Comic books / David M. Haugen, book editor.
   p. cm.—(Examining pop culture series)
   Includes bibliographical references and index.
   ISBN 0-7377-2545-1 (lib. : alk. paper)
    1. Comic books, strips, etc.—History and criticism. I. Haugen, David M., 1969– .
II. Examining pop culture.
   PN6710.C662 2005
   741.5'09—dc22
                                     2004054024

Printed in the United States of America

CONTENTS

Chapter 1: The Defining Elements of Comic Books

Chapter 2: Comic Books as a Reflection of Cultural Values

book agents fought America's enemies. They also championed the nation's economic superiority and democratic values.

often undercut by a legacy of social stereotypes. But some clever creators of black superheroes use this tension to fashion complex characters with realistic inner turmoil.

Chapter 3: New Forms for a Contemporary Audience

FOREWORD

POPULAR CULTURE IS THE COMMON SET OF ARTS, entertainments, customs, beliefs, and values shared by large segments of society. Russel B. Nye, one of the founders of the study of popular culture, wrote that "not until the appearance of mass society in the eighteenth century could popular culture, as one now uses the term, be said to exist." According to Nye, the Industrial Revolution and the rise of democracy in the eighteenth and nineteenth centuries led to increased urbanization and the emergence of a powerful middle class. In nineteenth-century Europe and North America, these trends created audiences for the popular arts that were larger, more concentrated, and more well off than at any point in history. As a result, more people shared a common culture than ever before.

The technological advancements of the twentieth century vastly accelerated the spread of popular culture. With each new advance in mass communication—motion pictures, radio, television, and the Internet—popular culture has become an increasingly pervasive aspect of everyday life.

Popular entertainment—in the form of movies, television, theater, music recordings and concerts, books, magazines, sporting events, video games, restaurants, casinos, theme parks, and other attractions—is one very recognizable aspect of popular culture. In his 1999 book *The Entertainment Economy: How Mega-Media Forces Are Transforming Our Lives*, Michael J. Wolf argues that entertainment is becoming the dominant feature of American society: "In choosing where we buy French fries, how we relate to political candidates, what airline we want to fly, what pajamas we choose for our kids, and which mall we want to buy them in, entertainment is increasingly influencing every one of those choices. . . . Multiply that by the billions of choices that, collectively, all of us make each day and you have a portrait of a society in which entertainment is one of its leading institutions."

It is partly this pervasive quality of popular culture that makes it worthy of study. James Combs, the author of *Polpop: Politics and Popular Culture in America*, explains that examining popular culture is important because it can shape people's attitudes and beliefs:

> Popular culture is so much a part of our lives that we cannot deny its developmental powers. . . . Like formal education or family rearing, popular culture is part of our "learning environment.". . . Though our pop culture education is informal—we usually do not attend to pop culture for its "educational" value—it nevertheless provides us with information and images upon which we develop our opinions and attitudes. We would not be what we are, nor would our society be quite the same, without the impact of popular culture.

Examining popular culture is also important because popular movies, music, fads, and the like often reflect popular opinions and attitudes. Christopher D. Geist and Jack Nachbar explain in *The Popular Culture Reader*, "the popular arts provide a gauge by which we can learn what Americans are thinking, their fears, fantasies, dreams, and dominant mythologies. The popular arts reflect the values of the multitude."

This two-way relationship between popular culture and society is evident in many modern discussions of popular culture. Does the glorification of guns by many rap artists, for example, merely reflect the realities of inner-city life, or does it also contribute to the problem of gun violence? Such questions also arise in discussions of the popular culture of the past. Did the Vietnam protest music of the late 1960s and early 1970s, for instance, simply reflect popular antiwar sentiments, or did it help turn public opinion against the war? Examining such questions is an important part of understanding history.

Greenhaven Press's *Examining Pop Culture* series provides students with the resources to begin exploring these questions. Each volume in the series focuses on a particular aspect of popular culture, with topics as varied as popular culture itself. Books in the series may focus on a particular genre, such as *Rap and Hip Hop*, while others may cover a specific medium, such as *Computers and the Internet*. Volumes such as *Body Piercing and Tattoos* have their focus on recent trends in popular culture, while titles like *Americans' Views About War* have a broader historical scope.

In each volume, an introductory essay provides a general

overview of the topic. The selections that follow offer a survey of critical thought about the subject. The readings in *Americans' Views About War*, for example, are arranged chronologically: Essays explore how popular films, songs, television programs, and even comic books both reflected and shaped public opinion about American wars from World War I through Vietnam. The essays in *Violence in Film and Television*, on the other hand, take a more varied approach: Some provide historical background, while others examine specific genres of violent film, such as horror, and still others discuss the current controversy surrounding the issue.

Each book in the series contains a comprehensive index to help readers quickly locate material of interest. Perhaps most importantly, each volume has an annotated bibliography to aid interested students in conducting further research on the topic. In today's culture, what is "popular" changes rapidly from year to year and even month to month. Those who study popular culture must constantly struggle to keep up. The volumes in Greenhaven's *Examining Pop Culture* series are intended to introduce readers to the major themes and issues associated with each topic, so they can begin examining for themselves what impact popular culture has on their own lives.

Comic Books: Reflections of a Changing Nation

LIKE JAZZ MUSIC, THE COMIC BOOK IS A DISTINCT-ly American creation. "It was born of American ingenuity, imagination, and old-fashioned capitalism,"[1] Mike Benton proclaims in his illustrated history of the comic book. Originating in the 1930s, comic books have stayed with America through economic depression, war, and political upheaval. Along the way comics, like any enduring art form, have changed with the fate of the nation. Sometimes prophesying the future, sometimes seeming to lag behind the present, comic books, however, have never lost their contemporary audience. Their popularity has endured in part because comic books are products of their times. Regardless of their ostensible subject matter, many comics reflect prevailing attitudes and the burning questions of the day. Patriotism in time of war, the liberation of sexual mores, the consequences of nuclear technology, changing male-female relationships, the connection between media and violence—all have been mirrored in the pages of comic books. And as America has matured, so have comic books. Once considered childhood diversions, comic books have now gained a more sophisticated readership as more adult themes and topics have found their way into what some prefer to think of as "graphic literature."

Origin of the Comic Book

While some modern comic books may strive to reach an older audience, the first comics aimed for the broadest appeal. In 1933 the Eastern Color Printing Company of Waterbury, Connecticut, decided to reprint newspaper comic strips in book form. The Sunday funnies pages were one of newspapers' most popular sections since they were pored over by both children and adults. Eastern Color executives tested the new format by convincing Proctor & Gamble to purchase ten thousand copies to be given away to customers who bought their products. The print run for *Funnies on Parade* was exhausted in a few weeks. Knowing they were onto something big, Eastern Color admen pitched similar offers to other manufacturers. This time a hundred thousand copies of a subsequent premium were printed and distributed. In addition, a few dozen copies of a ten-cent version were sold at various local newsstands. These disappeared almost overnight.

Over the next few years various collections of comic-strip reprints—such as *Famous Funnies, New Fun Comics*, and *New Comics*—were sold directly to the public in department stores and at newsstands. Their popularity brought other printing companies into the comics market. By 1936 six publishing houses were producing around seventy-five comic-book titles. The competition quickly forced publishers to offer new material in their comic books as well as the reprinted newspaper strips (although reprints remained the norm). In 1937 a collection of original mystery stories came out as *Detective Comics* #1. The following year the printer took over the rights to the series and created Detective Comics, Inc., which would become National Periodicals in a short time (and just as quickly would be renamed DC). The new company made history in June 1938 when it printed *Action Comics* #1, the first comic book to feature Superman, the world's first superhero. Superman was a novel creation, and his story lines, created by two youths named Jerry Siegel and Joe Shuster, were strikingly original despite being fairly tame. *Action Comics* and *Detective Comics* stood out from their peers because they presented original art and interesting characters. In the case of *Action Comics*, with the unique character of Superman, the formula brought success within the first five issues. A fantastic five hundred thousand copies of each issue sold from newsstands, and within two years Superman would be joined by a host of costumed colleagues.

In 1939 National Periodicals put out an issue of *Detective Comics* that featured a new comic-book champion called "the Batman" (or more commonly "Batman"). This caped crusader was an ideal foil to Superman because he was a mortal with no superpowers whose crime-fighting prerogative derived from a spirit of vengeance against the underworld. Superman and Batman defined the ends of the spectrum of comic-book heroes in the comic book's Golden Age (1938–1949), but in between would come a range of crusaders that ran from near clones to wonderfully unique creations. The Blue Beetle appeared in *Mystery Man Comics* in 1939 (published by Victor Fox), the Human Torch and the Sub-Mariner also surfaced in 1939 (for a new company called Marvel Comics), the Flash and Green Lantern arrived in 1940 (under National's newly renamed DC logo), and that same year Captain Marvel debuted in *Whiz Comics* (Fawcett Publications' first comic-book venture). All of these characters had to fight criminals and alien invaders to save the world (or at least their part of it), but their publishers had to face a more challenging foe—the economic ills that still plagued the nation in the waning years of the Great Depression—in order to survive.

If comic books are manufactured products as well as cultural products of their times, then it may be difficult to fathom how they were born in a time of national financial crisis. After all, the Great Depression cut across all classes, leaving only the richest Americans with luxury funds. Yet several factors conspired to not only keep comics afloat during the Depression but to make the industry skyrocket. The first was the comic book's price tag. At ten cents, the cost of comics was on a par with a trip to the movies. But unlike the movies, a comic book could be read again and again or traded to a friend for a different issue.

More important than the cost of a comic book, though, was its intrinsic value. Comic-book heroes at the end of the 1930s were champions of the dispossessed and downtrodden. As Bradford W. Wright, the author of *Comic Book Nation*, reveals, "In his initial episode, Superman saves a falsely accused prisoner from a lynch mob, produces evidence that frees an innocent woman on death row, and defends a woman about to be beaten by her husband." While these events mirror some of the common injustices done to the less-privileged classes, Wright goes on to illustrate how Superman was also used as a critic of the politicians and industrialists who were often blamed for the ills that had befallen the nation:

In the second issue of *Action Comics*, Superman crushes a

conspiracy involving a U.S. senator, a lobbyist, and a munitions manufacturer who wish to embroil the United States in a foreign war. He then ends the fraudulent Latin American war by informing the belligerents that they have been manipulated by greedy American industrialists. . . . Superman [then] warns that moneyed self-interest remained a menace to the national welfare.[2]

While adult readers responded to such messages, what resonated with children—especially young boys—was the rather giddy violence that pervaded early superhero comics. Superman fought crime by smashing his enemies, and any property that got in the way was usually written off as collateral damage. In the semirealistic world of early caped crusaders the operational philosophy was that the ends justified the means, and the real-world consequences of such actions were handily ignored.

Superheroes Go to War

When the United States entered World War II in December 1941, redirecting the violence in superhero comics toward real-world enemies was a natural and even patriotic move. The enemies were not only the armies of the Axis powers (mainly Germany, Italy, and Japan) but also money-hungry Americans who tried to make a profit from the war. As Bradford Wright explains, the welfare-state reforms of the 1930s—which had been championed by comic-book superheroes—were transformed by the advent of war. America no longer fought for the sake of national reform but reform on a global scale, so superheroes were called upon to rally Americans behind the war effort. Superheroes like Batman and Superman encouraged good citizens to buy savings bonds and conduct rubber, metal, and paper drives. Self-sacrifice coupled with wise consumerism was the key to victory. And that successful strategy would show the nation's superiority, making America a model for global change as the war progressed.

America's superheroes, however, still needed to clobber villains, so those who sought to turn the misfortune of war into an opportunity to make money became the nemeses of the crusaders who stayed on the home front. And the superheroes who took a more active role overseas sank Nazi submarines and crushed Japanese airplanes with glee. Don Thompson describes the unnatural joy Sub-Mariner took in battling the Japanese in one episode. Thompson writes,

> [Sub-Mariner] righted an overturned Japanese torpedo boat, rode it head-on into a destroyer, jumped overboard before it hit, salvaged a depth charge, and used it to sink an aircraft-carrier, machine-gunned some . . . landing parties, turned a flamethrower on them . . . , captured a submarine, brutally beat its commander, then torpedoed another sub. He laughed when . . . machinegun bullets riddled the submarine commander.[3]

Of course, this titillating violence was excused at the time because the Japanese were the enemy—and as such, they were stripped of their humanity and portrayed collectively as a devious, buck-toothed (sometimes fanged) menace that could easily be swatted with the least amount of superhero effort. The Germans suffered similar stereotyping but not one that was based on racial inferiority. The Germans were militaristic machines in the pages of comics. Most often exemplified by their tanks or by a lone Prussian officer who seemed equally brutal to his own men as to the Allied soldiers, Nazi power was technology married to an aggressive, martial pedigree. The whole German population was not evil (as the Japanese were portrayed to be), just the power-mad leaders and the militaristic aristocracy that had seized the reins of government and once again turned Germany into a military-industrial bulldozer. But even this bulldozer could be stopped by the American army—with a little help from Captain America, the Human Torch, Sub-Mariner, and other costumed champions.

The Atomic Age and the Cold War

When the Second World War came to an end in 1945, comic-book characters faced an uncertain future. While most superheroes returned to crime fighting, the postwar world would prove not as black-and-white as the wartime world in which heroes and villains were easily identified. Two Japanese cities had been eradicated by atomic bombs, and the impact would soon be felt throughout the globe. But between 1945 and 1949, America remained rather self-righteous. Still heady with victory, Americans initially conceived of atomic weapons as symbols of the nation's technological superiority. Children's comics of the times even incorporated atomic bombs into their slapstick arsenal, "sharing with cream pies and rubber hammers," history professor William W. Savage Jr. maintains, "the qualities of being uproariously funny and ultimately harmless."[4] More mature comic books were not much different. Even after the Soviet Union exploded its first atomic bomb in 1949—an event that ushered in the nuclear arms race—the superheroes, secret agents, and combat soldiers of American comics plodded through story lines that depicted America's atomic devices as far superior to the weapons of the nation's new enemy. Publications such as *Atom-Age Combat* and *Atomic War!* even printed bizarre parables about unwisely trusting in Russian restraint and the ultimate costs of not being prepared for a Soviet first strike.

Once the United States and the Soviet Union stockpiled enough nuclear weapons to make one-upmanship a moot point, the comics—like other facets of pop culture—settled down to tackling Cold War paranoia. Communist infiltration ranked among the most pervasive fears in America, especially after the trial of convicted spies Julius and Ethel Rosenberg and the rampages of Senator Joseph McCarthy, who conducted a witch hunt for "Reds" in politics, the media, and the military. As the search for fifth columnists occupied the national conscience in the early 1950s, authors of comic books had their superheroes and government agents consistently rooting out double agents and foiling the plots of Communist infiltrators. Once the Cold War heated up, though, as Communist revolutions spread into Southeast Asia, Africa, and Latin America, comic-book heroes were often called upon to save threatened democracies in far corners of the globe. In this tireless fight against the Red Menace, Savage notes that comic books were typically optimistic, "consistently assuming the swift and inevitable downfall of all Communist states, cells, and individuals."[5]

The only event to put a damper on the jingoism of the time was the Korean War. When the war began in 1950, the rapid success of the American and United Nations' intervention against the aggression of Communist North Korea seemed to illustrate Western supremacy. But when Chinese Communists entered the fray and pushed the Allied advance back, the war turned much bleaker. The change was reflected in the dozens of comic books with military titles that popped up in the war years. Soldiers in the comics with titles such as *War Fury* and *Two-Fisted Tales* were surrounded by death, and unlike the comic-book characters of World War II, these men ruminated on the horror and tragedy of the slaughter. Such tales were not inspiring readers to sign up and do their part; instead they made their audience aware of the grim lot of a soldier's life and the futility of fighting a war that seemed at times unwinnable.

Backlash

It was perhaps the grotesqueries of atomic death and the Korean War that nurtured the nation's new craze for horror comics in the early 1950s. William Gaines's Entertainment Comics (EC) was the flagship of the horror genre with titles like *The Crypt of Terror, The Vault of Horror*, and *The Haunt of Fear*. EC stood out from other publishers by writing for adult readers and never sparing the amount of blood, gore, and carnage that could be packed into the comics format. Coupled with EC's horror line were suspense titles such as *Shock Suspen-Stories*, which were also very graphic but dealt with everyday horrors rather than the supernatural. Some of these books examined racism, poverty, the court system, and other arenas where social justice had made few advances from the prewar years. The success of Gaines's venture proved that readers were ready for more thought-provoking comics in which the good guys and bad guys were seldom distinguished by costume.

By the mid-1950s EC's explicit comics inspired a host of copycats that had sprung up from independent publishers as well as major lines like Marvel and DC. Almost overnight, the deluge of bloody imagery became the target of moral crusaders. Chief among them was Fredric Wertham, a New York psychiatrist, who preached that American culture was obsessed with violence and the profane. In lectures given in the early 1950s and in a 1954 best seller, *Seduction of the Innocent*, Wertham maintained that comic books were awash with sex, murder, and destruction and therefore were contaminating the nation's youth. He and his allies believed that youth in the postwar years had an unprecedented amount of leisure time (enough time to read comic books), and much of that time was spent away from adult supervision. And oddly enough, this new youth culture seemed to arise at the same time that juvenile delinquency came to the forefront of media attention.

Putting two and two together, crusading adults, fretting over the growing independence of teenagers, lobbied Congress to launch investigations into the causes of juvenile delinquency in America. In 1953 a Senate subcommittee convened hearings on juvenile delinquency, and in April 1954 the subcommittee began its investigation of the comic-book industry. Wertham asked to give testimony on the corrupting influence of comics. As Amy Kiste Nyberg writes, "The committee took a very respectful tone with Wertham, allowing him to make a long statement before beginning its questioning; moreover, most of the questions were meant simply to clarify, rather than challenge, any of his testimony."[6] Following Wertham's speech, William Gaines read some words in defense of comic book publishers and their creations. His rhetoric was rather defiant, and his nervousness left him an easy target for a premeditated attack by the subcommittee members. Although other comics publishers spoke on behalf of their work, the industry as a whole presented no coordinated defense. The subcommittee adjourned to examine the evidence, but while giving no official pronouncement, several members made public statements that some form of regulation of horror and crime comics was needed.

Seeing the writing on the wall, the comic-book industry decided to preempt the subcommittee's judgment. In September 1954, Marvel, DC, and almost every other major publisher agreed to form the Comics Magazine Association of America (CMAA), a council of comic-book insiders who would act as a panel of censors for member publications. In October the CMAA printed a code that outlined how such delicate topics as crime, violence, death, profanity, nudity, and religion could and could not be illustrated or discussed. Every comic book issue had to adhere to the code in order to bear the association's seal of approval. EC and Dell Comics were among a handful of publishers that initially chose not to be part of the CMAA nor have anything to do with its code. Since it dealt with mainly kiddie comics that never contended with sex or gore, Dell opted instead to print and adhere to its own code to assuage parental doubts. William Gaines disbanded EC's horror titles and tried to launch other adventure comics. But because his products did not bear the CMAA seal, they were returned by distributors. Gaines eventually joined the CMAA, but by then his business was on the verge of going under, and in 1955 he would cease publishing comic books. Other publishers also went out of business due to the comics code, but EC, which had been so successful in the previous years, was the most notable casualty. Ironically, no legislation ever did arise from the Senate hearings.

Comix Counterculture

While the backlash against comics took its toll on EC, William Gaines was not out of the comics business altogether. In 1952 he had started printing a satiric comic book entitled *MAD*. After the fallout from the subcommittee hearings, Gaines decided to revamp *MAD* in 1955 and make it a comic magazine that focused on parody and satire. Despite its twenty-five-cent price tag, the irreverence of *MAD* caught on with an older readership that found life in postwar America less than idyllic. Surrounded by Cold War paranoia and the threat of atomic destruction, Americans wallowed in their creature comforts and social values. But even these were changing and provided no security; Americans took to buying more to feel better about themselves. "As the decade wore on," Maria Reidelbach writes in her history of *MAD*, "the situation grew only more intense. Conformity and affluence were supposed to bring ease and contentment, but Madison Avenue kept upping the stakes; there was no resting place in the climb to success."[7] Thus *MAD* poked fun at consumer culture, traditional values, and Cold War realities— revealing that the 1950s veneer of contentment hid an amalgam of absurdities. But as a satiric magazine, *MAD* did not offer viable alternatives to these social ills. Instead, it undercut its own position by consistently mocking itself and its readership. As Reidelbach writes, "If *MAD* encouraged the questioning of authority, it meant *all* authority, including its own."[8]

While *MAD* deflated mainstream culture, the typical comic books of the late 1950s and early 1960s were still of the superhero variety. Popular characters like the Flash and the Green Lantern held readers' interests, while in 1959 Supergirl made her first appearance. What distinguished Superman's cousin from her costumed comrades was that she was typically caught up in teenage romances instead of crime fighting. Indeed, besides superhero comics, teen romances and soap operas such as *Linda Carter, Student Nurse* and *Millie the Model*— both aimed at young female readers—helped fill the shelves of comics stands. Written under the restraints of the comics code, these major publications rarely dealt with challenging subject matter. In superhero books caped crusaders defended the status quo, and in romances boy-girl relationships resonated with gender stereotypes. By the mid- to late 1960s, however, the Vietnam War, civil rights protests, and college activism would change the moral landscape of the nation. The youth counterculture would spurn most tokens of mainstream America, and the simplified world of comic books seemed absurdly out of touch with the complex reality that more politically aware young people were experiencing.

While mainstream comics continued to sell well even in the turbulent 1960s, a breed of new artists and writers began creating comics for the disaffected counterculture. In 1967 *Zap Comix*, written, drawn, and sold by Robert Crumb, was the first of these publications to appear. *Zap* hit the streets of the Haight-Ashbury section of San Francisco in the following year. A counterculture and hippie enclave, Haight-Ashbury would become the nucleus of the underground comics (or comix) scene by 1969. Comix creators such as Crumb, Rick Griffin, Don Donahue, and Kim Deitch immersed themselves in the Haight-Ashbury atmosphere and fashioned stories about drug use, free love, crime, political corruption, racism, and any other "disreputable" topic that did not fit into the sanitized mainstream world. Author and comix authority Patrick Rosenkranz writes, "Underground cartoonists reflected their upbringing and environment. They were a generation weaned on television, comic books, and rock music, politicized by an Asian war and a generation gap five miles wide, and psychedelicized by lysergic acid [LSD]."[9]

Out of this admixture came a graphic style that was unfettered by the industry's comics code. The images were sometimes sexually explicit, sometimes violent, but always provocative. Occasionally, the small cadre of artists, writers, and printers had run-ins with the law, which deemed the material obscene (and in violation of federal legislation when sent through the mail to a subscriber), but any controversy remained minimal. Haight-Ashbury was a haven for misfit culture that routinely committed more serious violations, so, in comparison, the seizure of a few comic books never made the news. In addition, the limited print runs and homemade nature of these comix never threatened the mainstream comic book industry. Yet as Mike Benton asserts, "While the monetary impact of the underground comics on the industry was negligible, their influence as liberating pioneers would be widespread."[10]

Some New Ground, but Mostly the Same Old Story

Underground comix remained a vital force through the 1970s as the hippie movement shambled toward disillusion and dissolution. Another movement, however, grew to power in the wake of the 1960s counterculture. That movement was the women's movement, and it, too, had an outlet in comic books. Tired of the gender stereotypes professed in mainstream comics—especially romance comics, women artists and writers took their cue from underground comix and self-published works of their own. Dubbed "wimmen's comix" (or womyn's comix), these books dealt with gender inequality, workplace discrimination, child rearing, relationships (both gay and straight), and the daily drudgery of being second-class citizens in a man's world. Joyce Farmer, Lyn Chevely, Trina Robbins, Lee Marrs, and Delores Thom are but a few of the comics creators who borrowed from personal experience to produce unique publications that were eagerly snapped up by readers intrigued by this heretofore unrepresented female perspective. Like their underground kin, many of these publications lasted only a few issues, but their impact was noticeable. In the 1980s, for example, gay comics followed the path blazed by wimmen's comix in giving voice to a large, yet unrepresented segment of America.

Other than the advent of wimmen's comix, the early 1970s was a fairly quiet period for comic books. The innovative *Swamp*

Thing debuted, mingling gothic horror with the trendy ecological concern that gripped the nation. Otherwise, the 1970s witnessed the rebirth of defunct heroes such as Captain Marvel and the reappearance of genres such as the now-neutered horror comics. The lack of novelty may have been a result of a downsized industry. In 1974 only six major comic-book publishers—the fewest since the 1930s—remained in business. But those six—Archie, Charleton, DC, Gold Key, Harvey, and Marvel—produced a quarter-million titles that year. Of these publishing giants, Marvel and DC were the prize contenders fighting for dominance in the market. By the mid-1970s Marvel seemed to have the upper hand when it published the first issues of the new *X-Men* (a revamp of an older series), the title that has gone on to become one of the most popular and collected comics of all times. But the two companies typically parried each other's blows by imitating each other's new series. For example, when in January 1977 Marvel introduced Black Panther, its first African American superhero to lead his own series, DC shot back with Black Lightning within three months.

As Mike Benton claims, two of the most significant contributions to comics in the late 1970s were the advent of *Heavy Metal* and *Cerebus the Aardvark*. First published in 1977 by National Lampoon, *Heavy Metal* was a glossy magazine that collected and reprinted European comics. *Cerebus*, also appearing in 1977, was a small independent black-and-white comic book that followed the adventures of its aardvark hero. Besides containing excellent stories and crisp art by Canadian artist Dave Sim, *Cerebus* was important because it became the first independent comic book that maintained a steady publication through more than one hundred issues. This feat inspired a rise in independent comics that tried to mirror Sim's success. *Heavy Metal*'s influence was derived from the innovative visions of European artists whose attention to details and use of atmosphere would foster a legion of American imitators in the coming decade.

Reinventing Superheroes in the Age of Cynicism

The 1980s brought a new convention to the realm of comic-book culture. While comics were once sold exclusively at dime stores and newsstands, the early years of the 1980s witnessed the explosion of comic-book specialty shops. The shops survived by dealing with comic-book distributors directly and catering to a new collector's market in which comics buyers purchased one or more issues of the same comic book to store away in hopes that they would attain value in the future. The fans that hung around comic-book stores were also willing to browse and perhaps purchase independent comics like *Cerebus*. This development gave the independent movement a shot in the arm, prompting independent artists to take a chance with the new specialty market. The major players—primarily Marvel and DC—embraced the new, select audience in another way. Both started producing special series that featured many of their superheroes crossing over into each other's story lines. The idea was to prey on the "collectormania" that assumed such unique books would be prized possessions. Instead, the crossover gimmick (and other like-minded tactics) appeared regularly from 1984 onward.

The truly original stories to come from one of the major players appeared in the late 1980s. Frank Miller's *The Dark Knight Returns* and Alan Moore and Dave Gibbons's *Watchmen* both appeared in 1986 amid the normal plethora of DC titles. Both titles reconceived the superhero. Miller's tale is about Batman pulling himself out of retirement in modern times to fight old nemeses and return some level of meaning to his life. This older Batman is a twisted soul who is not a crusader of justice but a vengeful vigilante. Miller's Batman is a product of the violence that he combats, and therefore the character stands apart from the earlier kid-friendly incarnations of Batman. The dark nature of the short-run series appealed to more mature readers who enjoyed the malevolent take on a classic icon. Indeed, the significant aspect of *The Dark Knight Returns* was the way in which Miller deconstructed the hero stereotype—examining the internal struggle within a split personality and the real-world consequences of living in a society that prizes violence. Speaking of *The Dark Knight Returns*, Mila Bongco concludes that Miller's story was not the first to present a tormented character; rather "its novelty and consequent success lie more in the radical way it eroded the traditional superhero genre from within the genre."[11]

Watchmen is similar to *The Dark Knight Returns* in that it purposefully subverts superhero conventions. Alan Moore's story posits a world that seems an authentic mirror of the 1980s, but in this "real" world, superheroes exist. Unlike their more stereotyped counterparts, the superheroes in Moore's tale act and speak like normal people—except, of course, they are not. And because they are not, the government outlaws all superheroes except for the few who agree to work for the state. Of these, Dr. Manhattan is an atomic-powered mutant spawned by the government to do its dirty work. But after winning the war in Vietnam (this is a fictional story after all!) and beating sundry criminals, Dr. Manhattan feels no moral imperative to save humanity. When the new threat of a nuclear war between the Soviet Union and the United States emerges, Dr. Manhattan remains indifferent. Rorschach, another of the superheroes (though this one working as a renegade), does believe that nuclear conflagration deserves attention—not because of a sense of duty to humanity but because this character's world is one of absolutes in which evil must be vanquished. Rorschach is at turns vigilante and sadist. He takes satisfaction in destroying his foes but ultimately assumes that the human race is primarily wicked and not worth protecting for any moral reasons. Moore's skillful satire aims at questioning whether the world needs heroes. To him, heroes are often political constructions that inscribe values upon society and are therefore dangerous to freethinking. Like Miller's *Dark Knight*, Moore and Gibbons's *Watchmen* uses the comics format to examine the genre itself—asking significant questions about the purpose and function of superhero tales in society.

Miller and Moore were playing to the cynicism that seemed to pervade America at the time—especially among the young people who watched as news stories, movies, music, and other forms of media constantly called into question traditional forms of authority but could offer no alternatives. "Both *Dark Knight* and *Watchmen* . . . ," Mila Bongco argues, "comment directly on the post-Vietnam syndrome in the US with its ensuing loss of faith in the moral integrity of the State and its agents."[12] Yet neither text does more than "comment" on the decline; the audience is likely to leave the comic book feeling chagrined at the moral dilemma but remaining apathetic because the powers that be still appear dominant, in control, and unassailable. These feelings would come to define the so-called Generation X that came of age in the early 1990s.

Diversification

The issues of *The Dark Knight Returns* and those of *Watchmen* were collected into single volumes after their initial publication. As an anthology, *The Dark Knight Returns* spent thirty-eight weeks on the *New York Times* Best-Seller List. The new format heralded a trend in comics that would take hold in the 1990s. Realizing that collections of old comics issues could be repackaged in hard- and soft-bound volumes, comic book companies began producing these anthologies to sell to fans who may have missed the initial run of that story line. Soon bookstores as well as comic-book specialty shops were stocking the booklike anthologies and the new "graphic novels"—nonreprinted material that was structured as a book with more supposed literary pretensions than the average comic book. With book price tags and more mature narratives, graphic novels were (and still are) targeted at older audiences. They were an outgrowth of the "mature" lines of comic books that publishers like DC were experimenting with in the 1990s.

DC's first venture into mature comic books was the launching of the Vertigo imprint in 1993. In *Comic Book Culture*, Matthew Pustz writes, "Most of the Vertigo titles were written by British writers or women, and nearly all involved horror, the supernatural, or psychological science fiction."[13] Under the Vertigo umbrella, old DC series such as *Doom Patrol*, *Sandman*, and *Swamp Thing* were "updated"—meaning their characters spent about as much time musing on death as actually thwarting enemies. The line was pushed toward those college-aged readers who gravitated toward stories that were either gritty or gothic or both. Neil Gaiman's complete reworking of the Golden-Age *Sandman* was one of the most popular titles. With complex, metaphysical story lines that spread across several issues, Gaiman's tales, as Pustz notes, required the audience to have "a knowledge of history and literature"[14] to fully grasp the allusions and layers of meaning. And among this readership were a growing legion of female fans who appreciated the literary bent and the nonstereotyped women characters that shared equal time and space in the panels of Gaiman's work.

While *Sandman* and other Vertigo titles drew in a new audience, the independent market was burgeoning in the 1990s. Established independents such as Fantagraphics, for example, churned out a host of popular titles during the decade. More interestingly, though, many small presses (sometimes the artist alone) began using the new tools of a computer-literate society to produce comics that looked every bit as good as those from mainstream publishers. Technology liberated comics creators and allowed them to get their work out to the public with a minimum of investment. Meanwhile, the industry giants were still catering to the fans who cherished the traditional masked marvels, and many new series and crossover titles flooded the market. The zeitgeist of the comics scene in the 1990s was diversification. Comic-book shops held everything for everybody, but unfortunately, even this great outpouring could not sustain the market.

Decline

In the early 1990s Marvel began branching out into trading cards and other trendy licensing venues. The revenue generated by the sale of comic books, once the mainstay of Marvel, fell to less than 20 percent as the company diversified. But the balloon burst as the trading-card market fell apart, and Marvel neared bankruptcy before being saved by new ownership. The comic-book industry, which had reached $1 billion in sales at the end of the 1980s, watched as profits were cut in half by 1996. Marvel fared the worst because of its ill-fated venture, but DC also felt the blow.

Critics swarmed on the Marvel spectacle, arguing that the grand designs to become a licensing giant—the next Disney—left the comic books to suffer. Indeed, the industry-wide trends of the 1990s brought the quality of comics into question. Special poly-bagged collectors' issues, special issues marked #0 that come out after the series premiers, foil-embossed covers, and multiple crossover story lines drained readers' pocketbooks and left them feeling that the gimmick—rather than the adventure—was what they were paying for. Many readers spurned the comics for this reason, but it was not the only reason. The culture of the 1990s had changed in dramatic ways from previous decades. As Bradford W. Wright explains, "The last decade of the twentieth century saw a phenomenal expansion in the entertainment choices available to young people and a glutted market for adolescent obsessions."[15] Television and cable programming hosted fantasy shows that competed directly with the narratives of comics, and computer games and the Internet gave young people a more tactile experience of fantasy worlds than comics could convey. What kid wanted to read about superheroes when he or she could become a superhero in a three-dimensional video world?

At the turn of the millennium, comic books still remain one among many entertainment choices. The industry has not recovered from its slump, but that has not stopped the proliferation of new titles. Fans still eagerly await the next issue of *The Amazing Spider-man*, and the industry plods on, catering to its select clientele. The major players are also shoring up profits by putting a lot more emphasis on anthologies of old story lines. Repackaging Superman, Batman, and X-Men tales from the 1930s through the 1970s is the industry's way of capturing newer readers who do not have the time or financial means to acquire rare back issues. Nonmainstream publications are also still snapped up by their devotees. Especially beneficial for independent publishers is the dedication of whole sections of chain bookstores to graphic novels. There, Joe Sacco's *Safe Area Gorazde*, a comic-book narrative about life in war-torn Yugoslavia, has a chance to catch the eye of more sophisticated readers.

Perhaps the greatest expansion in comic-book retail, however, is the newfound fad for *manga*. The Japanese equivalent of the comic book, *manga* has literally exploded on the American scene thanks in part to the popularity of Japanese animated movies and television shows that have attracted young and old audiences alike. *Manga* stories have spun off television series (and vice versa), toys, collectible card games, and video games, so the current level of interest in this comic form is not likely to abate soon. Whether the fascination for *manga* will resurrect the industry as a whole is yet to be seen. Some critics believe the salvation of comics lies in crossing over to other media like the Internet. (Marvel has already experimented with comic-book series online.) Others argue that *manga* has pointed the way to broadening the international market and making more foreign comics available in the United States. But, perhaps, the future of comic books is best predicted by asking whether the culture still craves interesting narratives and art and whether Americans still need superheroes.

Notes

1. Mike Benton, *The Comic Book in America: An Illustrated History.* Dallas: Taylor, 1989, p. 11.

2. Bradford W. Wright, *Comic Book Nation: The Transformation of Youth Culture in America.* Baltimore: Johns Hopkins University Press, 2001, p. 11.

3. Don Thompson, "OK, Axis, Here We Come!" in Dick Lupoff and Don Thompson, *All in Color for a Dime.* New York: Ace Books, 1970, p. 128.

4. William W. Savage Jr., *Commies, Cowboys, and Jungle Queens: Comic Books and America, 1945–1954.* Hanover, NH: Wesleyan University Press, 1990, p. 17.

5. Savage, *Commies, Cowboys, and Jungle Queens,* p. 37.

6. Amy Kiste Nyberg, *Seal of Approval: The History of the Comics Code.* Jackson: University Press of Mississippi, 1998, p. 60.

7. Maria Reidelbach, *Completely MAD: A History of the Comic Book and Magazine.* Boston: Little, Brown, 1991, p. 182.

8. Reidelbach, *Completely MAD,* p. 188.

9. Patrick Rosenkranz, *Rebel Visions: The Underground Comic Revolution, 1963–1975.* Seattle: Fantagraphics, 2002, p. 4.

10. Benton, *The Comic Book in America,* p. 72.

11. Mila Bongco, *Reading Comics: Language, Culture, and the Concept of the Superhero in Comic Books.* New York: Garland, 2000, p. 170.

12. Bongco, *Reading Comics,* p. 143.

13. Matthew Pustz, *Comic Book Culture: Fanboys and True Believers.* Jackson: University Press of Mississippi, 1999, p. 84.

14. Pustz, *Comic Book Culture,* p.86.

15. Wright, *Comic Book Nation,* p. 284.

1

EXAMINING POP CULTURE

The Defining Elements of Comic Books

Combining Words and Pictures to Create Legitimate Art

David Carrier

Comic books are unlike most other visual arts because they combine pictures and a narrative tale into
a single artistic experience. In this way, they differ
from, say, illustrated literature in that the words and
images must be read together to understand the action and sequence of events. In the following article,
David Carrier describes how the aesthetic experience
of reading comics differs from examining a painting.
To Carrier, comics have a unique form of unity that
synthesizes words and pictures, allowing neither to
dominate the act of interpretation. As Carrier points
out, this characteristic has led to the more common
criticisms of comics as being neither true literature
nor self-contained visual art. But the "in-between"
nature of comics is just what, in the author's view,
makes them interesting, for it allows comics to be accessible and yet disconcerting—even provocative.
David Carrier is a professor at Case Western Reserve
University/Cleveland Institute of Art. He has written
several works about the visual arts.

SPEECH BALLOONS AND CLOSELY LINKED NARRA-
tive sequences—these are the crucial, the defining, elements of

■

comics. But there is a third way in which the comic strip differs in kind from other visual art. . . . Visual artworks, be they frescoes, panel paintings, or even old-master drawings, typically hang on walls. Spectators move around those objects. Movies, too, are public. Even when I am alone in a museum or movie theater, I am aware that others may enter this public space. By contrast, I read alone, without needing company or desiring that another person look over my shoulder. (Families who read aloud together create a kind of home theater.) Comics are read like books, by one person, who by turning the pages determines how fast he or she moves through the narrative.

The frames of old-master paintings function as a visual complement to the image. When, by contrast, many large modernist works are left unframed, that procedure says something about the informality associated with this art. . . . With the comic strip, the edge of the page functions like a frame. Comics, however, differ from both old-master and modernist paintings. In their admixture of image and word, comics are an in-between art—in scale, and so also in the relation they establish between viewer and object. Drawings may be as small as comics, but when framed and hung on museum walls, we respond to them as if they were paintings. . . .

Unity in the Visual Arts

Much is to be learned about comics by reflection upon the differences between the modes of attention demanded by this art form and those associated with painting and literature. [Philosopher Immanuel] Kant is concerned, [art historian and professor] Michael Podro notes, to explain what it means to say that "our experience is unified," considering "what powers of the mind must be posited in order to produce such unity"; "unity or order are not something that . . . could be provided by the material presented to the mind, but only something the mind itself imparts." The difficulty, Podro goes on to observe, is then to understand how it is possible to have any experience that is not in some nontrivial sense unified. . . .

An image has many identifiably distinct parts, so how can we both observe those individual elements and think of them as inextricably bound into one organic whole? Paintings are traditionally praised for their organic unity—for gathering a multitude of separate elements, so that no essential part is either superfluous or omitted, into one perfectly unified whole. Apart from monochromatic paintings, all pictures have many discrete parts—and even an apparently homogeneous monochrome has top and bottom, and left and right, sections. . . .

Art historians, accustomed to think of stylistic questions in empirical terms, are unlikely to find much aid in philosophers' abstract ways of talking about unity. Almost everything we see has parts, and so appeals to general conceptions of our synthesizing mental powers seem unlikely to teach much about what concerns the historian, the achieved unity, or relative disunity, of individual pictures. [Contemporary art historian Heinrich] Wölfflin's . . . practice suggests that art-historical judgments of unity tend to be comparative. It may be hard to characterize in so many words [Italian Renaissance painter Piero della Francesca's] unities, but comparing them with [Florentine painter Giotto di Bondone's] and Michelangelo's is suggestive; and contrasting all of these pictures to Chinese landscapes can help to identify their shared "Italian" unities.

Visual artworks employing both words and images raise different questions about unity. In Bible illustrations made around 1100, [Austrian art historian] Otto Pächt writes, "an inner contact between picture and script is never established, and the picture remains a cumbersome alien body in the book." What by contrast the ideal comic should provide is precisely such a contact between image and word, to the point that the two form an ideal unity. [According to J. Sparrow] "an inscription may be thought to be an alien and intrusive element in a picture"—intrusive because words and images differ in kind—and so it is natural to ask which, in any given comic, is more prominent. "The subordination of the pictorial to the literary," [British critic] Lawrence Abbott writes, "is one of the subtlest realities of the medium." Logically speaking, there need be no reason that the coexistence of words and pictures in a unified comic should cause problems. Just as a landscape painting can contain buildings, human figures, and landscape harmoniously set together without need for a hierarchy, so a comic book can bring together both words and pictures. But here, as with any binary opposition, it is natural to ask which element is more important. In comics, will words dominate pictures, or do words subordinate themselves to the visual component?

Words with Pictures or Pictures with Words?

Comics closely integrate words and pictures. Are they textual narratives with illustrations or, rather, pictures accompanied by texts? An argument for the former view might appeal to the fact that the comics can be paraphrased in words, as if they were novellas. So, for example, *Batman and Robin*, "What a Sweet Racket" (1 November 1943 to 7 January 1994), is the story of a missing convict who abducts Robin, fails to capture Batman, and is caught when Batman realizes that his own escape implicates a private detective who was secretly working with the mob. But such a paraphrase leaves out what is distinctive about this comic, the interplay of image and text. So, for example, in the introduction to this story we have description of the spotlight that "flashes a giant cone of light—etching an eerie symbol against the sky!"—and the bat-shape; and the action frequently depends upon visual devices, as when we read in a balloon the detective's hidden response to Batman's praise of his cleverness, "Cleverer than you think, Batman!" Paraphrasing a painting in words would leave out its visual elements, and (to some significant degree) the same is true with this comic. . . .

The only way of doing justice to any art form is to find its own proper descriptive terms. That comics combine these two different devices is one source of the feeling that they are an awkward in-between art, neither purely literary nor just entirely visual. Looking at comics, it is often said, is neither proper reading nor genuine viewing; too much attention to comics is thought to be bad for children, for it keeps them from learning how to do genuine reading. [Critic Ronald Schmitt argues,] "Two separate techniques must be employed by youngsters; two separate literacies." How appropriate that this in-between art form was invented by Rodolphe Töpffer, a would be painter who turned to writing and caricature because of problems with his eyes. What identifies the comic book for many commentators is its deficiency, its failure to be either a real text or just a proper image.

In *Seduction of the Innocent*, Fredric Wertham's famous moralizing critique of 1950s comics, the author complained about these in-between artworks: "Comic-book readers are handicapped in vocabulary building because in comics all the emphasis is on the visual image and not on the proper word." He is unwilling to think of reading comics as a special skill, different from, but not necessarily therefore lesser than, book reading. [Art historian E.H.] Gombrich has made this point in a more neutral way: "What I find very interesting is that so many half literate or illiterate can read the comics because they are combined with images. This combination is apparently much easier than either only images or only texts." Sometimes the felt problem with these combinations of images and words is that comics readers fail to learn to read properly. Comics undo knowledge of real reading: "those with good reading ability . . . are *seduced* by comic books into 'picture reading'" (my italics). Not surprisingly, Wertham objects also to another kind of what might be called in-betweenness encouraged, so he thinks, by comics—homosexuality. Looking critically at his claims, which had great practical effect on the comics industry, how striking is his reliance upon anecdotal information, without the pretense, even, of statistical argumentation: "It is true," he writes, "that many children read comic books and few become delinquent. But that proves nothing. Innumerable poor people never commit a crime and yet poverty is one of the causes of crime."

In 1946, Robert Warshaw complained that "the comic strip has no beginning and no end, only an eternal middle. . . . This . . . is a characteristic of Lumpen culture: all gradations and distinctions are broken down, even the distinction between art and life." Comics, as he described them, anticipate the painting of Robert Rauschenberg and Andy Warhol and much of what has been commonly identified as postmodernist art. More recently, writing in a similar vein, Robert Hughes has worried about how "the rapid negligence of Warhol's images parodied the way mass media replace the act of reading with that of scanning." Like Warshaw, he is concerned about what happens when the scanning of sequences of pictures replaces traditional reading.

No doubt Warshaw was correct to object to the nasty content of many of the comics of his day—the examples he cites are alarming; and Hughes certainly is right to have problems

Visual Narratives in Film and Comics

Since film and comic art developed simultaneously, artists in both media had to solve the same problems in visual narrative on their own and without the aid of established precedent. Therefore, one can find in early comic strips panels and sequences that are filmlike in their use of perspective and point of view. For example, uses of panning, in which the camera remains in one place but pivots to follow an action, were frequently employed by comic artists long before it became commonplace in film. Traveling or tracking shots, in which the camera moved with the subject, and close-ups or cut-ins, in which a portion of the previous scene is enlarged in the next as a point of focus, these too had their counterparts in techniques employed independently by comic artists. . . .

At their best, comic book artists carry the visual narrative into areas of innovation that the restricted camera cannot enter, except through animation, such as simultaneous continuities, or scenes that literally explode the strictures of the conventions of comic art. It is not surprising that student photographers and filmmakers now turn to comic books to learn the rudiments of their craft. The point here is that the mass market created for motion pictures by the film industry, which attuned audiences to stories told primarily through pictures, also looked to the other media for similar entertainment. Adventure and continuity comic strips, picture magazines, photogravure sections in newspapers, newsreels, and television were among the responses, but so was the comic book.

M. Thomas Inge, *Comics as Culture*. Jackson: University Press of Mississippi, 1990, pp. 143–44.

with mass-media images. But since such rebarbative content can also be found in much traditional literature and visual art, what is interesting about their complaints is the focus on how what might be called the formal structure of such images is threatening. Breaking down seemingly essential boundaries is often thought to be unnatural, and so morally pernicious, as is shown by the moralizing discussed critically in Tim Clark's social history of Impressionism:

> The boundaries between moral laxity and prostitution seemed to be dissolving, and this was held to be the more dangerous because it was not just sexuality that strayed over into the public realm, but money—money in fleshy form.
>
> The environs of Paris . . . were neither town nor country any more.

Women, whores or wives, whose role was hard to identify; parts of the city that were hard to place: they were felt to be dangerously disorienting. The once famous Villa Borghese *Hermaphrodite*, now in the Louvre, was said to cause visitors "to blush with pleasure and shame simultaneously" . . . [according to Francis Haskell and Nicholas Penny]. We expect the world to fit our preconceived stable categories, and so what falls in between is easily felt, depending upon our temperament and politics, to be either exciting or menacing. Hence the fascination with, and fear of, cross-dressing, androgyny, people of "mixed-race," comics, and other forms of in-betweenness.

To Tell One Story

A comic strip uses text and picture to tell one story—and so it is unified insofar as every element, visual and verbal, contributes to that end. Rationally speaking, why should there be any potential conflict between words and pictures when they work together to achieve that single end? A painting has many parts; a novel, many words; a comic, many images *and* words: we synthesize that multiplicity of elements to experience the artwork's unity. But we are not entirely rational, and so readily find something troubling about combinations of different arts. Roger Fry's perplexed description of what he believed was the inevitable lack of unity of opera displays this view: "[I]n so far as one was really interested in the drama, one began to be impatient at the slowness of the music, which, of course, was absurd, seeing that the only really important esthetic event was, so evidently, the music itself. . . . perfect co-operation between two arts becomes difficult in proportion as they reach a high pitch of intensity or completeness of expression." And the stage sets further divide our attention. Fry does not have any conception that drama, music, and sets could be working together to create one unified experience of the total artwork; for him, seeing an opera is like listening to a pianist while simultaneously a juggler performs nearby in front of a painting. The juggler and the painting would inevitably distract the audience from the pianist.

Synthesizing Separate Elements

In what Rensselaer Lee calls "the humanistic theory of painting," the goal was that of oratory, which "had been concerned not merely with words, but equally with gesture and facial expression as vital means of conveying human emotion." "As is poetry, so is painting"—according to the classical accounts these sister arts have similar goals, which they achieve in essentially different ways, painting displaying in a single image what poetry can reveal only in a narrative. If we take this tradition seriously, there is reason to expect conflicts in combinations of words and images. Insofar as such an artwork is visual, how could its all-at-onceness as picture be readily combined with its verbal narrative qualities? These classical ways of thinking, which do not do justice to modernist art, express still well-entrenched critical clichés that heavily influence how comics have been understood.

Once we acknowledge that all experience of art—whether reading literature or seeing pictures—involves synthesizing separate elements, why should comics and opera, which involve more than one kind of element, pose any special problem? If verbal and visual arts differ in kind, then they demand different, essentially opposed forms of attention. To look at a shape, viewing it formally, and to read a word involve essentially different, perhaps inevitably incompatible forms of attention. It is possible to evaluate a word aesthetically without knowing anything of the language. Fry admired Chinese paintings, enjoying "the graph of a dance executed by the hand." We all experience such defamiliarization when visiting an unfamiliar culture. Something may be learned about our own culture by learning how it is seen by an outsider. "I walk the London streets," a Chinese author [Chiang Lee] writes, "without any sensation of surprise at the shop-signs or advertisements in the windows, for they are almost all stylistically identical. They are neat, regular and symmetrical, but they are collections of lifeless letters." In China, by contrast, the corresponding advertisements are "an attraction to people of taste," who are calligraphy lovers. When in the European Middle Ages [according to Pächt] "objective representation [was] transformed into abstract ornament and reconverted into the former," words treated like images, a similar process occurred.

Immediate Experience Seems Undivided

If experience of words as words differs in kind from the experience of images as images, then how can images and the words in balloons and below the images ever constitute a genuine unity? A philosopher may here be tempted to draw an analogy with [philosopher René] Descartes's account of the unity of mind and body. Persons are unities of bodies and souls, things of distinctly different sorts that traditionally are given radically different value. Body and soul are linked in two ways: in action the soul moves the body; in sense perception, modifications of the body affect the soul. When I decide to act, I voluntarily move my limbs; when aroused erotically by what I see, imagine, or feel, my body is affected directly. In such situations my immediate experience seems to be undivided; only philosophical reflection suggests that the self might be composed of the two distinct substances Descartes identifies. The unity in comics of image and text is, ideally, as close a bond as this unity of body and soul bound together to form a person.

I mean this comparison of comics and persons as something more than an analogy. Comics, with their balloons, represent that relation of inner states and outward bodily expression which characterizes persons. Comics mimic in their narrative sequences that process which, if classical philosophy of mind is correct, characterizes perception. From a sequence of discrete individual sense impressions, philosophers have argued, we construct our world. Comics are personlike in their unity of words and images because they depict fictional persons whose actions are represented. Philosophical theories of the mind-body problem aim to explain that unity or to dissolve it. Comics merely illustrate this dualism, without taking any stand on philosophical questions about the nature of the mind-body relationship. In his account of Saul Steinberg, an artist who stands apart from, and yet is so close to, comics, [Arthur C.] Danto, speaking in terms familiar from his book on [French philosopher Jean-Paul] Sartre, notes that philosophers have "distinguished between the view we have of the world insofar as we are subjects of consciousness, and the view of us others have who perceive us as objects—between life as it is lived from the inside, as it were, and life lived in the recognition that we have an outside as well." The word balloon, by externalizing thoughts, makes visible the (fictional!) inner world of represented figures, externalizing their inner lives, making them transparent to readers.

Narrative sequence is for Danto a second feature of central importance in the structure of consciousness. He makes an analogy between this knowledge of other minds and what he calls "historical consciousness," which also "sees events as having an inside and an outside." To be historically conscious (in this broad sense) is to be aware of the immediate present as one of a sequence of moments, to "perceive both it and one's consciousness of it as something the meaning of which will only be given in the future." In externalizing this awareness, displaying the antecedents and consequences of one moment, comic-strip narratives thus show what it is to be a person. A cognitive psychologist who invented a working version of the ring of Gyges—permitting us to look into the minds of others and see their inner thoughts—would but duplicate the balloons in comics. Reading these narratives is to look into the minds of the fictional characters, as if their inner worlds had become transparent to us.

The assumption shared by those who like and those who dislike comics is that they are a mixed art form, part word and part image. The problem of the medieval illustrator, Pächt writes, was "reconciling the requirements of pictorial space

with that of the painted surface of the page of the book."
Comics, it might seem, should be understood similarly. A
product of mass culture, they use popularized versions of images from traditional visual art, supplemented with words to
serve as easily accessible narratives for semiliterate audiences.
Movies serve that same public, but they are a genuinely novel
invention, the product of truly original technology; comics, by
comparison, are inherently a compromise visual art form.

Conventions of the Superhero Narrative

Mila Bongco

In the following selection, Mila Bongco examines
some of the themes and literary characteristics found
in most superhero comics. To begin with, Bongco
places comic books in the realm of heroic fantasy adventures in which "tough and honourable" protagonists confront a problem or obstacle with violence.
According to Bongco, women are typically helpless,
and the male-centered order is always reestablished
after some elaborate fisticuffs on the part of hero and
villain. What the author finds interesting, though, is
that many superheroes are outcasts who operate outside the laws, the same laws that they inevitably uphold by vanquishing evil. In fact, the hero's need to
work outside the establishment amounts to an implicit critique of the police and legal institutions. After covering this transgressive dimension of comics,
Bongco goes on to illustrate common motifs of the
genre and the lack of strong female characters in a
world of hypermasculine bravado. Mila Bongco is the
author of *Reading Comics: Language, Culture, and the
Concept of the Superhero in Comic Books*, from which
this selection is taken.

AT THE HEIGHT OF ITS POPULARITY IN THE EARLY
1940s, the superhero comicbook was a unique visual phenom-

■

Mila Bongco, *Reading Comics: Language, Culture, and the Concept of the Superhero in
Comic Books*. New York: Garland Publishing, 2000. Copyright © 2000 by Mila
Bongco. All rights reserved. Reproduced by permission of Routledge/Taylor & Fran-
cis Books, Inc., and the author.

enon. In most cases, it was in a standard 64-page magazine format and celebrated the exploits of superheroic characters in action-packed, vividly coloured covers that children found hard to resist. The superhero dominated the pages of the early comicbook. These were mostly muscular men in brightly coloured tights shown performing remarkable feats of strength and defeating strange villains one after another. The heroes also had all the traits a child could dream of: speed, strength, power, and knowledge. The recurrence of this sight and theme in the minds of thousands of children and adolescents over a fifty-year period must have helped the American (male) youths to a better understanding or recognition of their fantasy goals as they related to their personal ideals. Interestingly, what primarily appealed to the visualised fantasies of childhood provided the twentieth century with a pantheon and mythology comparable to those of previous cultures. The superhero figure has developed into a lasting and vigorous presence in American and European popular culture such that the recognition of the Batman or Superman, for example, by millions who have never read a Batman comicbook or seen a Superman film is ensured.

The lasting popularity of superheroes is rather unexpected if we consider the characteristics most familiar to superhero comics: a) the plot, characterisation, and theme are relatively simple; b) they rely frequently on formulaic plots and traditional symbols; c) there is an interpreting narrator to direct the stories; and d) simple, cartoon-like illustrations with bright, primary colours are used. While their generic similarities and obvious evocation of archetypes make them easy to remember, most superhero texts seem to be quite undetailed. The stories are so similar to each other, possess very few qualities distinct enough for durable impressions, and do not seem substantial enough to allow permanence over the years. Yet, despite their sameness, superhero comics have endured, have crossed over to other media, and have managed to maintain their almost worldwide presence in popular culture. Closer scrutiny of the genre reveals that the persistence and popularity of certain superheroes and particular texts belie the seeming interchangeability of these comicbooks. In fact, thousands of devout comicbook fans could enumerate differences in detail that would quell any doubts about the uniqueness of each text. Then again, careful analysis of the particulars of these "differences" shows that they are often appreciated in relation to their unexpectedness or deviance from a recognisable convention of a superhero text. This enjoyment derived from the manipulation of established conventions indirectly acknowledges the existence of a "model" or a "paradigm" for such texts. . . .

Formulaic Narratives

A logical place to start in ferreting out the characteristics of the superhero narrative is in scrutinising its two most apparent features: the hero and his adventures. For this purpose, John Cawelti's description of the basic structure of a hero's adventure is very useful, pertinent to the point that it begs to be included here:

> The central fantasy of the adventure story is that of the hero . . . individual or group . . . overcoming obstacles and dangers and accomplishing some important moral mission. Often, though not always, the hero's trials are the result of the machinations of a villain, and, in addition, the hero frequently receives as a kind of side benefit, the favours of one or more attractive young ladies. However, the interplay with the villain and the erotic interests served by the attendant damsels are more in the nature of frosting on the cake. The true focus of interest in the adventure story is the character of the hero and the nature of the obstacles he has to overcome. This is the simplest and perhaps the oldest and widest appeal of all formula types. It can clearly be traced back to the myths and epics of earlier times that have been cultivated in some form or other by almost every human culture. At least on the surface, the appeal of this form is obvious. It presents a character with whom the audience identifies passing through the most frightening perils to achieve a triumph. Perhaps the most basic moral fantasy implicit in this type of story is that of victory over death, though there are also all kinds of subsidiary triumphs available depending upon the particular cultural materials employed: the triumph over injustice and threat of lawlessness in the western; the saving of the nation in the spy story; the overcoming of

fear and defeat of the enemy in the combat story. While the specific characterisation of the hero depends on the cultural motifs and themes that are embodied in any specific adventure formulas, there are in general two primary ways in which the hero can be characterised: as a superhero with exceptional strength or ability or as "one of us"—a figure marked, at least at the beginning of the story by flawed abilities and attitudes presumably shared by the audience.

Seen against this basic hero formula, the construction and appeal of the comicbook superhero become obvious and apparent: being pure fantasy, it can cover all kinds of fantasies and triumphs enumerated above that evoke the mythical and span the range of themes from moral conflicts to combat stories. Furthermore, superheroes embody the two types of hero mentioned since they are usually endowed with a dual identity being simultaneously a super-power while also being "one of us." Superhero narrative is simple and formulaic, held together by rapid action of one such character or a group of such characters. A mystery or dilemma is confronted with violence. Women are victims to be rescued. Heroes are tough and honourable. The law needs the hero's help. There are elaborate fight scenes whose winner is almost inevitable. Language is masculine. Plotting is precise and often predictable. Dialogue is short and punchy until the elaborate schemes of the villains need explaining. The conclusion is foreseeable. But despite the predictability of the stories, for some inexplicable reason, the "willing suspension of disbelief" in readers becomes inexhaustible. No matter how many times Superman, the Batman or Spider-Man achieve their triumphs, the next adventure captivates again, and reader suspense and involvement is always successfully manipulated. The play between predictability and innovation must account for some of the reading pleasure in the texts, and may lead one to the conclusion that the form is not as restrictive as is often thought.

Disruption of Normalities

Classic superhero narratives usually start with a disruption of the status quo and proceed to a discovery and eradication of the perpetrator of this disruption. Usually, the "establishment," namely, the police, and the judiciary, are the forces given credit for restoring order and stability, since the Superhero usually works with them. In classic superhero fiction, the disruption takes place in closed hierarchical communities—a "named" and identifiable, albeit imaginary, locale like Metropolis and Gotham City. The problem is solved by the superhero who is generally known as an establishment figure. The comicbook ends with the restoration of the old hierarchies. The superhero from this position could thus be seen as the last bastion of imperialism and outmoded class attitudes, sanitised violence, racism, sexism; he has too much respect for authority and an unhealthy tendency to see moral issues in absolute terms. However, attributing to superhero narratives such conservative forms tends to imply rather negative reasons for the prominence or persistence of the genre among its readers. It would suggest that its readers are those attracted most by repetitive genres with conservative implications.

But this view is erroneous. It is based on a too scanty knowledge of the history of superhero comicbooks, and a far too rigid interpretation of the superhero genre, at least an outdated one in view of the more recent re-makes of many of the genre's characters and narratives. More and more, one can assert that the boundaries of the superhero are relatively fluid. This genre does not necessarily have conservative implications since only an extraordinarily fertile and productive genre could have spread and caught the attention of readers worldwide for so long. It is true that classic superhero texts tended to end with certainties—chaos is vanquished and stability is restored. In the past, the classic superhero figure also tended to be an establishment figure which seemed to imply that the forces of law and order were always good and unproblematic. Nevertheless, it is possible to make a convincing argument that the outcome of the fights is often only secondary to the unfolding of the disruption and its effects, the ensuing confrontation with the villains, and the development and expansion of the superhero character in each issue. Even in a "classic plot" involving rather uncomplicated protagonists, there are at least two problematic elements: a) the depicted society is always in danger and its institutions for law enforcement are deficient, otherwise it would not need a superhero; and b) the restoration of peace and order is only temporary since recurring threats to a superhero's domain are intrinsic to the genre. In some cases, popular protagonists are even deliberately left to escape and their probable return is implied. In addition, many superheroes operate outside the law—the Submariner, the Hulk, Plastic Man, the Spirit, and countless others—helping powerless and worthy people to defend themselves against criminal and evil forces in areas where the official system of law and order has proven ineffective. The ending is moreover usually perfunctory, a necessary ending, but hardly equivalent to the complex fight scenes, the elaborate illustrations and interactions which preceded it, as well as to the flamboyant and memorable villains and rogues who litter superhero narratives. In reaching the end, all sorts of unexpected things can happen just as all sorts of unexpected things are introduced. After all, crime involves the disruption of normalities (superheroes themselves are already a disruption of normalities), and superhero narratives are often the consequences of this disorder. While the plots are naturally geared towards the restoration of law, they are also about the breaking of the law, about the transgression of normal rules. Viewed from this perspective, the narratives become more interesting and take on more dimensions especially in relation to power and control. It is possible to perceive the genre as actually dealing with the transgression of the law, portraying the play between breaking and restoring law, or at the very least, showing an ambivalence about law and order. After all, if the police were efficient and sufficient in maintaining law and order, superheroes would be unnecessary. The presence of superheroes to augment the establishment's capacity to uphold the law lends a distance between the hero figure and aspects of [the] establishment. Moreover, the superheroes of today have evolved a great deal from the unabashed patriots of the 1940s and 1950s. Since the early 1970s, they have been shown routing out scientists, politicians, priests, and other establishment figures who turn out to be in league with criminal elements. With the sophistication of the more recent graphic novels, the once reassuring form of traditional binary oppositions and simple disputes in the older texts have given way to a multitudinous and pluralistic range of images that fit our contemporary existence. Newer texts like *The*

Dark Knight Returns, Watchmen, Astro City, and *Madman* tackle complex moral dilemmas and diverse political shifts where changes and contradictions cannot so easily be labelled and appraised. Often, the superheroes themselves question their role in upholding the law in a world where those in powerful and institutionalised positions have debatable intentions and morality. The world is very different from that of thirty years ago: the bases of power have shifted, and so have ways of understanding them. Old certainties have gone, though new and perhaps equally repressive authoritarianisms have emerged. These, in their turn, must be challenged. This present world of uncertain directions and kaleidoscopic and contradictory images is increasingly reflected both textually and visually in comicbooks.

Innovative Superhero Trials

There is one other essential feature of usual adventure or hero stories that is used quite differently in superhero tales: these are the trials designed to test if the hero should really be a hero, if he is a match for the tasks set before him, if, for example, he can cheat and triumph over death. But superheroes were conceived to be intrinsically indestructible. That a superhero never dies is a tacit agreement between artists and readers for otherwise, there would be no subsequent issues of that comicbook. The superhero's immortality, however, is directly [in] proportion to its popularity which then dictates which comicbooks will be further published. Such narratives are not really geared towards an innovative ending other than the hero's triumph. The innovation and variability of each text is actually in presenting a variety of villains and in cooking up the "distortion" of the law. The originality and creativity of the artists lie in making up and developing transgressions that provide the plot in each issue. In a way, it is actually crime and the supervillains that keep the superhero in business. The proliferation of crooks and chaos is allowed as long as core ideas of the origins and identity of the hero are maintained. Committed comicbook readers have come to expect this, and letters to the editor often applaud or rebuke these "innovative repetitions," implying that the readers accept some rules governing story-construction and superhero definitions. . . .

Staple Motifs of the Genre

The concept of an invulnerable character with superhuman strength caught the fancy of a nation as Superman's arrival created a whole new genre out of a very coarse set of materials. Today, many aspects of the first Superman and its narrative approach have the appearance of a cliché. Indeed, much of what would become central to the superhero genre was already established in the thirteen pages of the first Superman issue. The first issue introduces readers to a distant, dying planet and explains that a "scientist" placed his infant son in a spaceship, launching it towards Earth. The "sleeping babe" is discovered and delivered to an orphanage (Clark Kent's parents were a later addition to the mythology). On reaching maturity, the young man discovers he has considerable powers (though modest compared to the god-like capabilities that he would later acquire in his fifty-year career). He decides to dedicate his strength to the service of mankind, and becomes Superman—"Champion of the oppressed, this physical marvel who has sworn to devote his existence to helping those in need." All these facts were contained in just the first page. The next five pages relate how Superman prevents an innocent woman from going to the electric chair, how Clark gets an assignment from the (yet unnamed) editor of the *Daily Star* (later to be renamed *Daily Planet*) and assigned to cover the feats of Superman, and how Superman intervenes in a wife-beating scene.

Then, as Clark Kent, he meets his colleague Lois Lane who agrees to a date to "give him a break, for a change." It was a disastrous date, interrupted by a challenge to fight from a "hunk" called Matson who disdains Clark's pacifist attitudes, and later bundles Lois Lane into his car as she angrily leaves the club by herself. The car's getaway was blocked by the imposing figure of Superman who tips both Lois and the roughnecks out of the car, and then trashes the vehicle (this is the panel which provides the subject matter for the first *Action Comic*'s famous car-throwing cover). Clark's problem, in that his second identity steals the affections of Lois, starts here; the very next day, Lois treats him more coolly than ever. Meanwhile, Clark is assigned to stir up news for the *Star*'s front page and is told to go to the small South American republic of San Monte. But instead, as Superman, he takes the train to Washington to investigate corruption in the US Senate.

The actions and motifs in this first issue reveal the influence of usual hero-adventure narratives, as well as establish much of what will be staple to the superhero genre. Some of the features that would be repeated countless times in other superhero stories could be listed as follows: a) aberrant or mysterious origins, b) lost parents, c) man-god traits, d) a costumed, secret identity, e) difficulties with personal and emotional relationships, f) great concern for justice, and g) use of superpower in politics. Similar to Superman being forced to leave Krypton, the usual superhero adventure begins with someone from whom something important has been taken away—home and/or family, a loved one who dies, normal human constitution because of an accident, the sense of security is threatened, the feeling of complacency is lost because of the awareness of a "difference," and so on. In the usual hero-adventure story, the hero then undertakes a mission to recover what has been lost, to avenge a wrong, to discover some life-giving elixir or all of these together, usually fulfilling a cycle of departure and return.

For the true superhero, this cycle is rendered impossible by the nature of their "repetitive narratives," not to mention commercial demands, which dictate that they should battle again and again and thus bar any return to a former, calmer existence. The superhero cycle is simply comprised of discovering the cause of disorder and defeating the transgressor. However, even the ensuing peace and calm is often illusory, contradicted by an intrusion from the comicbook editor who advertises the next issue(s), directing the readers to upcoming battles and cancelling any pretence of a complete cycle.

Struggling Toward Autonomy

Another basic motif of hero adventures utilised in this genre is the departure from one condition, usually psychological immaturity or physical dependency, in order to achieve individual and communal success. As in the folktale world, a superhero's coming into his inheritance or the acceptance of his "difference" and consequent role in society may be seen as a symbol of coming to a condition of moral autonomy. One favourite technique in obliging superheroes to confront autonomy is the loss of parents or a loved one—the Batman, a.k.a. Bruce Wayne, is haunted by the murder of his parents; Superman hails from a dying planet and is raised by human foster parents; Spider-Man's closest relative is his Aunt Mary who is also murdered; Wonder Woman starts as a lifeless sculpture created by her mother and she later renounces her immortality to remain in this man's world; the Submariner lost both his parents in a clash between humans and the inhabitants of Atlantis; Daredevil starts working out to avenge his father's death.

Although heroes in the folktale and comicbook worlds may be said to be already earmarked for great deeds, many superheroes are different from folktale heroes in that their status is not gained by undergoing trials and tasks; most of them start out as a result of freak accidents (Spider-Man, Captain America, Dr. Manhattan, the Fantastic Four, the Hulk) or they are born somewhere else which gives them special powers on Earth (Superman, Wonder Woman, Mighty Thor, Iron Man, Submariner). Through no conscious desire of theirs, they find themselves thrown into an advantageous or extra-ordinary position. Some possible exceptions are Daredevil and the Batman who decide to transform themselves physically and mentally, driven by vengeance for their parents' murder. In dedicating over twenty years of his life to changing his physical and intellectual prowess, the Batman achieves what other superheroes already possess: some special powers that are either physical, magical, attributable to a weapon or device, or, most frequently, a combination of the above. We must not forget that supervillains may also have certain powers and the motivation to be supreme. What separates the two types of superbeings is the moral triumph that drives the hero in contrast to the egotism of the other. The implicit high moral[ity] of these avenger-type heroes provides a critique of the customary institutions of law and order in society, and expresses a desire for a fiercer and purer authority that would arise to punish evil, without the delays and corruption of constitutional law. In varying degrees of severity and explicitness, the presence and polarity of superheroes and the superhero genre involve a critique rather than a celebration of a given society's judicial system. If society does enjoy a distinct and central power source, then why the need for aberrant heroes? The code of the superheroes reveals a transcendent sense of justice that throws into question the accepted civil justice and the nature of "law" itself. As each superhero takes the "law" into his own hands, an alternative sense of justice is presented which implicitly or explicitly problematises the nature of "law." Acceptance of laws and social order should negate any need for independent crimefighters who are sometimes adversial to both state police and criminals.

That superheroes usually want to remain unknown to both crooks and cops attests to a preference not to favour (or trust) either side. A superhero has to assume another identity or an alter ego for reasons of privacy and protection. Having to assume dual identities, however, usually means entering into a series of compromises, learning to be selectively deaf and blind to inconvenient realities. This may sometimes prove problematic for the superhero's alter ego because, whether in his private or "public" life, readers have come to expect a high morality in the superhero character. . . .

Female Tropes

In comicbooks, characters are drawn according to a highly coloured and simplified scheme, and female characters were in general more loosely imagined than men and less invigorating to identify with. There were few major roles for women within the pages of such magazines. Most females are "girlfriends" of the hero and serve two functions: trying to learn the hero's identity and always getting into trouble so that the hero has someone to save. Or, they wear skimpy outfits, thus producing what is termed as "good girl art" in the comicbook community:

> Good Girl superheroines of the 1940s operated in the wider context of the Vargas pin-up girls, the Just Jane cartoons and sweethearts of the forces such as Betty Grable and Rita Hayworth. Good Girl art takes the signs of pornographic discourse (whips, chains, spiked heels, beautiful but blank faces) and integrates them into the context of non-pornographic story structures. In this way, the sign of pornography (never explicitly delivered) comes to stand in for an entire pornographic sub-text, a series of blanks which readers remain free to fill in for themselves. And it is within the neo-pornographic texts of Good Girl art that the dis-

tinctions between costumed heroes and villains can first be seen to break down, a change that in turn influenced mainstream superhero comics. [Richard Reynolds, *Super Heroes*]

The "girlfriends" of the superheroes are always portrayed as well-behaved, alert and intelligent. Nevertheless, they are also marked by extreme vulnerability to harm and hopeless infatuation. This theme was already present in the first issue of *Superman*, and Lois's obsession with the superhero continues today. But although Lois has lived just as long as Superman, she has never achieved equal star status in comicbooks. The pages of comicbooks abound with unflattering clichés about women's powerlessness and isolation which in turn provides a reason for the superhero to come to their aid. Lead female characters in more current comicbooks are portrayed to be more aggressive and more dangerous—for example, Vampirella and Lady Death—but in general, the ideology remains the same.

This common theme crosses over to both heroines and female villains, blurring the boundaries between them. There are many female antagonists who are shown to be victims of their circumstances as women, and later atone and change over to employing their superpowers at the service of justice. Catwoman started as a well-known Batman adversary, in the league of the Joker and Penguin, even conniving with the Batman's enduring foes. She is revealed to have been a streetwalker who turned to crime partly to help those in the same plight and others oppressed by poverty. Although she still works outside the law and is often wanted by the police, she now leans more and more towards being a superheroine than a villain. Spider-Woman, like many other superheroines, started outside the law as Hydra, an agent for an unknown spy organisation, under threat of death. As her powers increased, she became a superheroine who was featured in her own comicbook. Many of Wonder Woman's female enemies turn out to be under hypnosis or under somebody else's power, usually that of a male scientist. A featured villainess who appeared in a series of Wonder Woman comicbooks, Baroness Von Gutenberg, was only acting for the Nazis because they kidnapped her daughter. The Baroness had to be helped out of this hostage situation and thereafter became Wonder Woman's ally. Red Sonja enjoyed super-powers because she hailed from the majestic kingdom of Hyrkania which she was forced to flee after her parents were slain and she spurned the advances of the pillagers' king and slew him.

Male Dominance and Female Reduction

Especially in the early years of comicbooks, it seemed that women could not be portrayed as extremely evil as some male villains were. There are hardly any female antagonists who remain as vile and unscrupulous throughout their comicbook career as some well-known male villains. Although by the 1950s, many sultry and hard-hearted female villains were created in reaction to the honourable and competent women of earlier comicbooks and strips, there was neither conspicuous menace in their intentions nor gruesome violence in their adventures and fight scenes. During the years from the 1950s to the early 1960s, there were many heroines who adopted the aggressive, face-smashing attitudes of their male predecessors—instead of a man bursting through the door and executing an impressive jumpkick to his adversary, it was a woman. But in spite of some sympathetic, independent heroines and some socially satisfying plots, their acceptance of the individualistic and machismo codes of violence were highly problematic. Most of these heroines were conceived by men, drawn mostly by men, and targeted for male adolescents, resulting in "good girl art." The comicbook industry was so dominated by men for so long and so little attention was paid to the polysemy of comicbook texts that most of the differentiation of female characters remained in the visual level; the code, message and way of thinking were clearly male and simply transposed into the mouths and minds of heroines.

The "reduction" of female protagonists may also be seen in the usual underestimation of their capabilities by both policemen and crooks. The intervention of female heroines seldom seems to evoke the deference from lawmen or terror from criminals (regardless how reluctantly) that herald the arrival of male superheroes in critical situations. Similarly, a female antagonist has yet to create a distinct and memorable response of fear or loathing among the superheroes the way the Joker has, or Lex Luthor, or even J. Jonah Jameson. By extension, women in general have been relegated to minor roles in superhero texts, and presented in ways that give priority to men and the idea of adventure; women have their assigned places in the men's lives and are made secondary to what passes between a man and other men. Women provide motivations for the men's great deeds, but superhero texts eschew the idea of intimate relations with women.

Letters Pages Foster Community

Matthew Pustz

As Matthew Pustz points out comic books are one of the few pop culture art forms that allow fans to interact with the creators and each other in dialogues that can have meaningful impact on the progress of the series. This forum for discussion takes place in the letters pages (or letters columns) of each comic book. Here, readers can debate fine points of the characters and the narrative and—if the comic's creator is receptive—make suggestions as to how the storyline will continue in future issues.

In the following article, Pustz outlines the distinctions between letters pages in mainstream and independent comics. He also acknowledges how the fan responses run the gamut from gushing praise to abusive criticism. The minute details brought up and hashed out in the letters pages exemplify just how seriously many readers take this unique form of literature and art. Finally, as fascinating and revealing as letters columns are, Pustz cautions that these pages are always a mediated form of fan-author/artist interaction since the comics creators decide which letters to print and which to dignify with a response. Matthew Pustz is a regular reviewer of comics for PopMatters.com. He is also the author of *Comic Book Culture: Fanboys and True Believers*, from which this viewpoint is taken.

■

COMIC BOOKS MAY BE A MARGINALIZED FORM OF popular culture, but their fans have one distinct advantage over those of other forms of popular culture. In comic books, there is always the potential for fans to interact in sites published, and hence made official, by the creators responsible for the production of the texts themselves. This kind of interaction takes place in letters pages (also called letters columns or lettercols) included in most regularly published comic books. These letters pages can be an important source for research into the culture of comic book readers, but they must be approached with care.

As Martin Barker warns in *Comics: Ideology, Power, and the Critics* (1989), "Letters are selected, and often for early editions solicited or ghostwritten. They are not produced by some 'natural sampling' of readers' responses". This manipulation by publishers makes letters pages so useful: "They are a part of the self-image of the comic. They present that self-image, and help to encourage the right kind of future response from readers". Letters thus can reveal editors' ideas about a comic's intended audience and about how it will be read. These pages are also important because they allow fans to interact with creators, content, and other readers. This is one of the most basic levels of interaction in comic book culture, where participation is so widespread that it helps to make it unique among popular media cultures.

Fostering Community

As comic books grew in popularity in the early 1950s, publishers began to transform a text page mandated by postal regulations from an infrequently read short story to a compilation of readers' comments. William Gaines's EC Comics was one of the first companies to prominently feature these letters pages on a regular basis. In its horror comics of the early 1950s, these pages were "hosted" by that title's narrator: the Crypt-Keeper, the Vault-Keeper, or the Old Witch. Fans could make announcements about clubs, advertise for pen pals, comment on stories, argue with other fans, and participate in contests to see who could invent the most disgusting pun along the lines of those offered at the end of the stories. Along with the "Fan-Addict Club," the lettercols were crucial in creating the brand loyalty—and the sense of community—common among EC's fans.

By the early 1960s, letters pages had become a central part of comic book culture and constituted a crucial ingredient in the origins of an organized comics fandom. The practice of printing writers' complete addresses enabled fans to communicate directly with fellow aficionados and to compile mailing lists of people who might be interested in fanzines. Publishers also used the letters pages to mobilize fans. Marvel Comics in particular used the lettercols to create a sense of community and loyalty among its fans. Letters columns in *Fantastic Four*, among others, were filled with in-jokes, praise for fans, and, most important, a sense of shared adventure that made early Marvel readers feel like participants in the company's success. Fans were proud to say that they were "True Believers," and the letters pages were important in creating this feeling.

DC and Marvel Distinctions

By the 1970s, nearly all mainstream comics included letters. There were, however, important differences between the lettercols published by DC and Marvel. In many DC comics, letters were shortened, excerpted, or compiled into lists of suggested guest stars. Marvel letters pages, conversely, often contained very long letters in which fans praised, criticized, or offered detailed suggestions. Unlike DC editors, who referred to readers as "them," the editors of Marvel's letters pages frequently directly addressed their fans, often using the inclusive "we" or "us." The letters page in *Captain America*, for example, was called "Let's Rap with Cap"; in *Daredevil*, it was called "Let's Level with Daredevil." This phrasing suggests a kind of mutual participation among creators, editors, readers, and even the characters themselves. Around this time, DC featured lettercol mastheads depicting some of its characters reading fan letters. The contents of the letters pages, however, contradicted these visual messages, as editors often deliberately separated creators from readers. Marvel's readers were encouraged to suggest story ideas, as editors emphasized the close ties between the audience and the creators. The idea that fans—as editors in absentia—and professionals were creating the comics together was central to Marvel's rhetoric. Many fans undoubtedly believed they had a role in shaping their favorite comics and, perhaps as a result, the company became the most successful American comic book publisher by the late 1970s.

Along with this variation in tone and strategy, there were also important differences between Marvel and DC letters in terms of subject matter. In the 1970s fans writing to one of the DC titles would almost always comment on a previous issue's story, either praising or panning it. Fans writing to Marvel comics would do the same, but substantial numbers of people also examined comics' content by offering interpretations of long story lines or explanations about the powers and abilities of various supercharacters. Negative letters were common in both Marvel and DC letters pages, especially in the 1970s, but the criticism often differed. While Marvel fans' criticism could be very pointed, focusing on the work of particular writers and artists or even the company's whole output, negative letters from DC fans were usually mild, comparing a weak story to a stronger one a few issues earlier. Very rare were wholesale attacks on the company or even a particular series. By the early 1980s, though, DC letter columns began to become more like Marvel's, with longer letters that privileged content and commentary over simple reaction. By the late 1980s and early 1990s, Marvel letters pages had lost much of their critical edge, with DC lettercols taking up the slack.

Letters pages can also be found in contemporary independent and alternative comics. There, they often serve different purposes than in mainstream comics. The letters pages in *Hate* and *Naughty Bits* both establish and nurture a sense of community among readers based on generation and gender, respectively. Letters can fill up nearly half of each issue of Dave Sim's *Cerebus* because of fans' long-winded responses to his stories and their political implications. Dan Clowes uses his occasional letters pages in *Eightball* to mock his less psychologically stable fans and mirror the comic's sense of irony and weirdness. Other alternative creators use lettercols to rant about their lives, political and cultural issues, and the comic book industry.

Laudatory Letters

Lettercols in all sorts of comics encourage interaction between fans, content, and creators. On the most basic level, this interaction occurs in the letters of commentary, the most prevalent type of fan correspondence. Readers are clearly not afraid to shower their favorite creators with effusive praise. *Sandman* fan Cris T. Halverson of Minneapolis wrote, "Thanks to all of you [involved with the comic] for bringing to us the most artistic and profound thought-provoking comic ever (and the only one to hold my attention). Special thanks to [the creators] for unsurpassedly bringing such life and depth to characters that have existed before and beyond humankind and [the] comics realm. My wholehearted agreement with all those impressed and obsessed who have praised you in the past, and I'll leave it to those yet to come to voice the rapture in my marrow each time I pick up or set down yet another issue" (*Sandman* #32 [November 1991]). This kind of praise could be found in Marvel comics of the 1960s and early 1970s, too, where creators had become heroes themselves. Writer Steve Englehart was a favorite of many Marvel fans, especially for his work on *Dr. Strange* and *Captain America*. One reader, Thomas Holaday of Wellesley, Massachusetts, was so excited by Englehart's work that he declared that the writer "is scripting the most *contemporary* fiction in America," adding that the details "convince the reader that he is in the midst of a special kind of genius, the kind that knows the roots, stems, leaves, and blossoms of the Tree of Popular Knowledge" (*Captain America* #183 [March 1975]). Fans also get excited about the kinds of stories that a writer or artist tells. Readers of Terry Moore's *Strangers in Paradise*, for example, have praised his depiction of women. Fan Debbie Byrd enthusiastically announced that this is "a comic for women!" filled with authentic images of women's lives: "You won't find any triple-E silicone-filled busts bursting from a shredded t-shirt conveniently torn to reveal just enough flesh to get a guy breathing hard here," she writes. "What you will see are sweat pants and tousled hair, sagging breasts and bulging bellies" (*Strangers in Paradise*, v2 #1 [April 1994]).

Laudatory letters in Marvel comics have traditionally gone beyond praising the creators to celebrating the publisher as well, especially for its supposed courage and relevance. These letters often mimic Marvel's own self-congratulatory prose. One fan applauded a handful of creators for "daring to be different, daring to experiment, daring to be GREAT. THEY ARE DARING TO BE MARVEL!" (*Alpha Flight* #16 [November 1984]). Dwight Halberstam of Denver waxed philosophically about the upcoming death of a member of the team: this event and other Marvel births and deaths "show us what it is that makes Marvel so special: change. . . . As in real life, nothing is constant in the Marvel Universe. . . . It is wrong to think of the Marvel Universe as somewhere else, somewhere governed by different rules, different causes and effects. The Marvel Universe is OUR universe. Those heroes live HERE, on OUR earth. It is OUR lives they protect, our values they represent" (*Alpha Flight* #16 [November 1984]).

Critical Commentary

The lettercols include more than just praise, though, as fans have often seen through the lack of quality in their reading. Particularly during the 1970s it would not have been difficult to find negative responses in comics' letters pages. Some are simple complaints about a story or art. Other letters can involve a great deal of anger, especially when fans believe that a character is being mishandled. Writer Denny O'Neil's infusion of "relevance" into DC's *Green Lantern* was generally praised, but some readers were angry about the comic's new political emphasis. "Surely *Green Lantern* deserves a better fate than to be made the tool of an ideological extremist," one fan wrote. "Just as I would not have William Buckley write *Green Lantern*, so too do I object to Mr. O'Neil's opinionated, fustian rhetoric. His gall seems to know no bounds. The decade-long work of [writers John] Broome, [Gardner] Fox, and others in establishing *Green Lantern* at the pinnacle of comic magazine perfection has been completely nullified in three short issues by Mr. O'Neil's propagandistic extravaganza" (*Green Lantern* #81 [December 1970]).

The murder of Spider-Man's girlfriend, Gwen Stacy, in the early 1970s prompted some bitter and angry letters from fans. J. M. Black of Alameda, California, wrote, "HOW DARE you kill Gwendolyn Stacy!? You are a pack of soulless, mercenary sadists. I am no longer a True Believer." Sergio J. Andrade, of Roselle, New Jersey, was perhaps even angrier, addressing his letter "to whomever had the idea of killing off

Gwen Stacy": "You rattlesnake, you buzzard, you large red insect, you worm, you cockroach, you lizard, you skunk, you tapeworm in the digestive system of humanity: why is it when a superhero and his girl finally seem to be getting it together, you kill off the girl? May you lose every tooth in your head but one, and in that one may you have a toothache; may someone put arsenic in your midnight cocoa; may you, be struck down by a spirit of justice and be reincarnated as an amoeba!" (*Amazing Spider-Man* #124 [September 1973]).

Fans of alternative comics sometimes react angrily, too. Many readers of *Hate* were dismayed, to say the least, by Peter Bagge's decision to print the series in color. Some suggested that it was a sign that he was selling out, while others claimed it was no longer as "edgy" as it once was. One fan explained, "I used to love the visual aspects of [Bagge's] comix, it created the perfect atmosphere, and indulged my eyes. Now *Hate* looks like a piece of shit, like something that should be in the Sunday comics. BRING BACK THE REAL DRAWING AND PUT AN END TO THIS CRAP! I am (or was) a faithful reader of *Hate*. . . . Now you have lost me" (*Hate* #19 [June 1995]).

Creators Respond

In the 1970s Marvel editors frequently tried to placate angry readers by explaining how important their letters were to the company. Some reiterated [Marvel creator Stan] Lee's notion that readers' letters were important as guidelines for the creators. Responding to complaints about *Power Man*, one editor explained, "We don't score hits with every issue. Sometimes, a story has flaws or just doesn't come up to snuff. Which is why your letters are so valuable to us in producing these comments. . . . So don't let anybody tell you your letters aren't important, people. They are vital to these magazines" (*Power Man* #24 [April 1975]). Fifteen issues later, the message was the same. "We actually *do* read every letter you send" the editor claimed. "We listen to your comments. We write and draw our books according to what you—the *real* editors of Marvel Comics— want to see. How else do you think we became the number one comics company today?" (*Power Man* #39 [January 1977]). The emphasis on this kind of relationship in 1970s letters pages differed greatly from Marvel's approach in the preceding decade. During the company's early years, Marvel created a sense of camaraderie in the pages of its stories. By the 1970s, though, whether because of bad or overly serious comics or because the comics failed to reach the anticipated audience, that kind of rapport—or the illusion of that rapport—had to be established in the letters pages, subtly changing their purpose in Marvel's overall strategy regarding its readership.

Creators involved in independent and alternative comics often explain their goals for their letters pages at the beginning of a new series. Some artists and writers are clearly interested in creating accurate samplings of feedback from readers. In the second volume of *Strangers in Paradise*, Moore announced, "I will make a point to run all kinds of comments [on the letters pages], not just the lovey stuff. Since *SIP* is a story about the good and bad in life, it only follows that the letters column should read the same way and not like a lettercol from a fanboy magazine" (*Strangers in Paradise*, v2 #2 [November 1994]). Other creators are less hospitable. Martin Wagner, author of *Hepcats*, declared, "It's my humble opinion that if you don't like me or my work you don't have to be [in the lettercol]" (*Hepcats* #0 [November 1996]). . . .

Questions About Content

Questions from readers and the resulting responses from creators or editors are essential for the development of a unique letters page. Most of these questions focus on a handful of themes. Many fans try to point out mistakes or logical incongruities within stories. Other mainstream readers ask about continuity, especially where a story fits into the overall history of a superhero universe. Some want more details about characters: for example, the letters pages of Kurt Busiek's *Astro City* are filled with questions about characters of whom readers get only a tantalizing glimpse. Busiek refuses to answer, urging his readers to be patient and wait for the story that will resolve their questions. The letters pages, then, give readers a forum for discussing their theories about his often mysterious characters.

Discussions such as these shift reader interaction on letters pages to the realm of content. Often, these missives are very specific, centering on events themselves. Other letters focus on the intricacies of plot, with writers sometimes offering their own ideas for where a particular story line should go or suggesting scenarios for new stories. Some reader interaction with content focuses on characters. Fans of comics that combine two or more heroes flood the letters pages with suggestions for costars, while team comics attract letters filled with ideas about new members. Many fans are particularly sensitive about a character being portrayed accurately, prompting letters filled with tips for writers and artists on how to depict the "real" hero.

Some interaction with the content of comics functions on a broader level, though, when readers offer their own interpretations of stories or use them as inspiration for discussion of other topics. Some reader interpretations are simple analogies, finding parallels between comics events and those in the real world. Fan Greg Jones, of Houston, Texas, for example, saw the Galactus story as a symbol for American involvement in Vietnam, with the Silver Surfer representing the United States (*Fantastic Four* #54 [September 1966]). Other interpretations are more like literary analysis, especially in DC's Vertigo comics, where complex systems of symbols and multiple layers of meaning inspire readers. . . .

Political issues are among the many topics fans address in letters pages. Paul Chadwick's 1996 miniseries, *Concrete: Think Like a Mountain*, involves the encounter between the title character, a former political speechwriter whose brain was transplanted by aliens into a nearly indestructible body, and members of the environmental group Earth First! By the end of the six issues, Concrete has joined their organization and helped to save a virgin forest in the Pacific Northwest from loggers. Taking a cue from the content of the story—and from the creator's announcement in the first issue—the letters pages were filled with a conversation between Chadwick and his readers about the morality of Earth First!'s tactics and environmentalism in general. Not surprisingly, a vigorous debate ensued, with some readers announcing that the series had actually politicized them to the point of action (*Concrete: Think Like a Mountain* #4 [June 1996]).

Fan-to-Fan Dialogue

Letters pages also give fans an opportunity to interact with each other. Some of this interaction involves debates between fans over content. For example, Dave Olsen of Santa Barbara, California, wrote "an open letter" to a number of prominent Legion of Super-Heroes fans whose correspondence had been urging more developed relationships between members of the group. "If you want ROMANCE, why don't you stick to romance comics?" he asked. "Personally, I appreciate it when a comic is what it claims to be; and after all, this *is ADVENTURE* Comics. Please remember that" (*Adventure Comics* #353 [February 1967]). . . .

Other fans have come together in support of their favorite titles through letters pages. In the mid-1970s, Marvel's *Amazing Adventures*, starring a swordsman named Killraven in an apparently hopeless battle against an invasion from Mars, always seemed to be under the threat of cancellation. As part of a campaign to save the comic, fan Mason Aldrich urged his fellow readers to "get off your tails and write today! Or the next copy of *Amazing Adventures* you receive may feature Millie the Model" (*Amazing Adventures* #36 [May 1976]). The campaign was short-lived, however; the comic was canceled three issues later. According to his letter printed in the final issue, Aldrich received seventy letters in the span of a week and a half supporting his effort to save the publication, with many thanking him directly for his efforts (*Amazing Adventures* #39 [November 1976]).

Happier interaction also takes place in the letters pages, as fans share their own creations. One issue of *Astro City*, for example, contains a photograph of fan Paul Saint-Laurent's homemade action figure of Busiek's hero, Jack-in-the-Box (*Kurt Busiek's Astro City*, v2 #6 [February 1997]). *Strangers in Paradise* (v2 #1 [April 1994]) ran a contest in which readers were asked to send their portraits of the main characters, Katchoo and Francine, with the best poetry and artwork published in subsequent issues. In the letters pages of *Hate*, Bagge ran contests that awarded readers dates with characters and special appearances in the comic (for example, the "Win a Date with Stinky" contest [*Hate* #3 (fall 1990)]). A different kind of creativity could be found in Bongo Comics's *Radioactive Man*. Some fans developed their own scenarios to fill gaps in Radioactive Man's past, while other readers strove to point out "continuity errors" within the existing issues (*Radioactive Man*, v3 #216 [August 1994]). This interaction helped to expand the mythos of the series and make the humor, at least in the letters pages, a collaborative effort.

Fans of the Legion of Super-Heroes also worked with creators through lettercols to construct a fantasy world. Readers chose team leaders in letters, and some suggested new characters appear in the comics. Other readers simply had questions about the futuristic universe where the Legion's adventures take place. The answers from editors and creators helped to make that universe more realistic and three-dimensional for fans. . . .

Importance to Comics Culture

Because of all of this interaction, letters pages occupy an important place in comic book culture. Lettercols exist at the boundary between fans and creators, readers and content; the fact that it is an official and public forum makes the interaction there unique. Television programs and movie stars receive mail from fans, but those letters rarely become public. With comic books, though, fans interact in the publications themselves. This interaction may occur in isolation from the rest of the media world, but it only helps to intensify the boundaries created in the process. Fans gain an identity and have it strengthened through awareness of others involved in similar activities. This awareness—and the feeling of fellowship it creates—begins in the letters pages.

Still, it is important to remember that the letters pages offer readers a site for *mediated* (if not manipulated) interaction. Editors decide which letters to publish and which to ignore; some editors create their own letters to serve their own purposes. Without further research, it is impossible to tell how much of the interaction is real and how much is a kind of public relations effort on the part of comic book publishers to educate their audience about how the comics should be read. The reality of letters pages is most likely somewhere in between authentic expressions and cynical manipulations. Even if the lettercols are based primarily on the imaginations of comics readers, the communities that result are important, as is cultural participation through letters pages. Without lettercols, comic book culture might not exist at all.

EXAMINING POP CULTURE

Comic Books as a Reflection of Cultural Values

Comic Books During World War II: Defending the American Way of Life

Ian Gordon

American comic-book heroes became involved in World War II before the United States did. In 1940, Sub-Mariner, a Marvel superhero, was fighting Nazi U-boats that threatened to close off the shipping lanes between North America and the United Kingdom. Over the succeeding months, as America was increasingly drawn into the European conflict, comic-book battles came to U.S. soil. Superheroes had to turn their attention to spies and saboteurs bent on crippling U.S. military stores—many of which were being sent to Britain's aid. When Japan, an ally of Germany, attacked America in December 1941, comic-book superheroes were finally unleashed to take on the nation's foes overseas as well as at home.

In the following article, Ian Gordon, the head of the history department at the National University of Singapore, discusses the role comic books played in the American war effort. Comics were one of the preferred reading materials of U.S. servicemen, and therefore publishers printed stories that extolled patriotism and the importance of fighting for democ-

■

Ian Gordon, *Comic Strips and Consumer Culture, 1890–1945*. Washington, DC: Smithsonian Institution Press, 1998. Copyright © 1998 by the Smithsonian Institution. All rights reserved. Reproduced by permission.

racy and the American way of life. Although some superheroes and other comic-book characters did fight enemy forces on the battlefields of Europe and Asia, many of the most powerful remained stateside. As Gordon points out, heroes like Superman could have theoretically defeated the enemy single-handedly, so comic-book writers had to find ways to keep the most omnipotent heroes at home.

Confined to the home front, many superheroes continued to fight enemy spies and fifth columnists, but they also became models of everyday patriotism. Superman and Batman promoted war bonds and lectured on conserving needed war materials. Yet, as Gordon explains, the comic-book stories of the time also showed an American society virtually untouched by the war. The implicit message was that good citizens would lead normal, consumer lives in wartime. It was the American way of life—which was in part based on the freedom to spend money and keep the economy strong—that would help the nation prove its superiority in the global contest. Superheroes supported this outlook by taking time out from fighting enemy insurgents to tackle dishonest businessmen or criminals who sought to wreak havoc on American industry. The overriding belief was that maintaining economic well-being during the war would lead to prosperous postwar years for the nation.

BETWEEN 1941 AND 1944 SALES OF COMIC BOOKS doubled from 10 million to 20 million copies a month despite paper shortages. Much of this increase can be attributed to the reading habits of servicemen. In 1944, 41 percent of men between the ages of eighteen and thirty read comic books regularly, which researchers defined as more than six comic books a month. In military training camps, 44 percent of men read comic books regularly and 13 percent read them occasionally. Female readership of comic books, which from ages six to seventeen was only 4 to 6 percent less than male readership, dropped to 28 percent for women between eighteen and thirty.

At age thirty-one and over the difference between male and female readership returned to 4 percent. In that age-group 16 percent of men and 12 percent of women read comic books. The disparate rates of male and female readership between ages eighteen and thirty suggests that military service, predominantly a male activity, led to increased comic book readership.

John Jamieson's semiofficial account of the Army's Second World War Library Service attributes a general increase of readership among soldiers to boredom. The Army operated a library service in order to maintain morale. As Jamieson put it the alternatives were apathy, discontent, drunkenness, and a soaring rate of venereal disease. As part of its attempt to provide soldiers with a regular supply of reading material, the Library Service organized a set of magazine subscriptions for companies posted overseas. In 1943, when this system proved cumbersome, the service began the centralized distribution of an overseas magazine set. The *Superman* comic book was one of the eighteen titles in this and the only comic book. Through 1943 and early 1944 the Army distributed at least 100,000 copies of this comic book every other month, or about 10 percent of the comic's sales. The Army dropped *Superman* from the magazine set in 1944 because it was readily available at post exchanges. Comic books outsold the combined circulation of *Reader's Digest, Life*, and *The Saturday Evening Post* by a ratio of ten to one at these exchanges.

Popularity with Servicemen

Comic books were one of the most regular contacts overseas servicemen had with America. In 1944, as a result of the Soldier Voting Law, the War Department determined the magazines for which soldiers had shown a preference through paid subscriptions and readership. Comic books accounted for over a quarter of the 189 soldier preference magazines. A major in the Southwest Pacific combat zone observed the precious status of comic books among the men on troop transport ships. U.S.O. hostesses noticed that comic books were the first items to leave their tables. A photograph in *National Geographic* of a soldier with a pile of comic books showed that servicemen accumulated large numbers of the books, and officers reported that they passed among men until they fell apart. . . .

Comic books owed their popularity among soldiers to a number of obvious features. They were cheap, easy to read, and light to carry, But two other factors probably contributed to their ubiquitous presence. First, the extraordinarily high prewar readership of comic books by young males may have given them an iconic status during the war. In owning and reading comic books, soldiers likely possessed a small part of what they fought for. Such an explanation parallels the war correspondent John Hersey's report that the Marines on Guadalcanal fought the war for "a piece of blueberry pie," "scotch whisky," "dames," "books," "music," and "movies." It also echoes the sentiments of an American soldier who wrote home that he fought to maintain the right to drink Coca-Cola.

Not Always Easy to Recognize the Heroes

Some of the comic book heroes were too powerful to turn loose on mere human (or, if you prefer the wartime propaganda, subhuman) opponents. Superman, for one, steered clear of the war for the most part, with a lame excuse about how Our Boys didn't really need any help. The real reason, of course, was that Superman couldn't enter the war without ending it immediately—and, obviously, the war wasn't ending immediately.

The less-than-omnipotent superdoers could fight the Axis, however, and most did, both at home and abroad.

None threw themselves more fully into the fray than the heroes of the outfit known variously as Timely, Atlas and Marvel Comics. Their wartime heroes, particularly the Human Torch, the Sub-Mariner, and Captain America, fought the most elaborate plots, with no holds barred.

The casualties on both sides were tremendous—the complete obliteration of some European or South American country (or city) such as Holland (or Buenos Aires) was passed off by our heroes as a minor setback. Regi-

Robert Westbrook has recently demonstrated that pinups served as iconic representations of soldiers' private obligations to the war effort through their evocation of a generalized American womanhood in need of protection. Comic books may also have echoed pinups as reminders of home and like them given the individual soldier a reason to fight. Second, comic book story lines accounted for their standing among soldiers. Many comic books contained witless tales in which American forces easily defeated their foes. But the most popular comic book characters, Superman and Batman, appeared in stories set exclusively on the home front. These two characters both supported the war effort and protected American society from its domestic opponents. As well as reminding sol-

ments of German and Japanese soldiers were wiped out at a blow, by floods and explosives.

It is hard to believe, in these days of racial tolerance and played-down violence—particularly in the comics—but it was a common sight to behold the Human Torch burning the arm off a grotesquely deformed Japanese while a pretty girl gleefully cheered him on.

The Japanese all wore glasses and had buck teeth (or, often, fangs) and long claw-like fingernails. Their skins were usually yellow, often greenish-yellow. Reference to their racial inferiority was common—they were the Enemy, so it was all right to derogate them racially.

It was not always easy to recognize the heroes during the war years, except by noting who came up smiling at story's end. The heroes gloated so much over the maiming and killing of the Enemy that they seemed far more villainous than the villains. They were supposed to be better looking than the bad guys, but the art wasn't always good enough to make that clear.

Don Thompson, "OK, Axis, Here We Come!" in Dick Lupoff and Don Thompson, eds., *All in Color for a Dime.* New York: Ace Books, 1970, pp. 121–22.

diers of home, the content of these comic books probably helped reinforce the purpose of the war in their minds.

Superheroes Aid the War Efforts

Comic books from DC were the most popular of the war era. Part of this success was due to the company's identification of Superman and Batman with the war effort, which established them as defenders of an American way of life. In the December 1941 issue of *Action Comics*, the "Supermen of America" page said readers could express their confidence in the U.S. government "and the Principles of Freedom and Justice and Democracy" by purchasing U.S. Savings Bonds or Stamps for Defense. The message from Superman stressed that, although young people could not hope to purchase bonds, defense stamps could be had "for as little as twenty five cents." The column also urged readers to "do a little salesmanship job on the older folks."

This bond promotion was part of a campaign by Henry Morgenthau, secretary of the Treasury, "to use bonds to sell the war, rather than vice versa." In a radio address during the spring of 1941, Morgenthau explained that there were quicker and easier ways for the government to raise the money than through bond issues. But the Treasury had decided "to give every one of you a chance to have a financial stake in American democracy—an opportunity to contribute to the defense of that democracy." Once the United States entered the war, Morgenthau continued the bond program to give civilians a sense of participation in the war effort. . . .

Most wartime issues of DC's comic books carried an advertisement for war bonds and stamps. These promotions of war bonds made Superman and Batman salesmen for the war effort and suggested that a democratic society was something citizens could buy their way into. Furthermore by 1944 a large number of adolescent comic book readers had money to spend. A census survey of April 1944 revealed that one in five schoolboys ages fourteen to fifteen had jobs, as did two in five sixteen- to seventeen-year-olds. By the latter age 35 percent had left school and were working full-time. Girls were not as likely to be employed, but of sixteen- to eighteen-year-olds a third had jobs.

Detective Comics, Incorporated's promotion of war bonds was part of an intensive national campaign to sell the war that encompassed a variety of businesses and practices. Many businesses promoted war bond purchases. Entertainment industry figures lent their celebrity to bond drives. The singer Kate Smith sold $40 million of bonds in a sixteen-hour radio session on September 21, 1943. The Hollywood starlet Loretta Young sold bonds at a Kiwanis meeting, and the pinup girl Betty Grable auctioned off her stockings. Moreover the bond campaigns fit with the convergent thinking of the advertising industry, government, and consumer advocates on the notion of citizens as consumers.

Promoting Responsibility on the Home Front

Beginning in 1939, with George Sokolsky's *American Way*, the advertising industry consciously depicted consumer choice as a constituent element in and guarantee of political democracy. Advertisers had associated advertising and consumption with American values throughout the 1930s, but Sokolsky's book raised the conception to an ideology of "the American Way." During the war the industry's War Advertising Council acted as a clearinghouse for both the government's and private industry's wartime propaganda. Much of this advertising addressed citizens as consumers, urging them to cut back on their consumption of goods and cooperate with government measures to increase war production. The consumer advocate Caroline Ware saw responsible consumption as a "contribution to the war effort.". . .

A September 13, 1943, advertisement in the *Los Angeles Times* for *Popular Science* warned, "Keep your shirt on, America"; too many saw Victory as "too close, too easy." *Popular Science* advised Americans that they could count on "better stuff, or better materials" but not to "count on them too soon." A life insurance industry advertisement published in the *Times* on September 9, 1943, listed seven practical steps to build a "*personal* post war world." The first step was to buy war bonds, the second to pay taxes, the third to buy life insurance. The overall message was to spend less and save more. The ad suggested that "good American families" understood that even though war production put more money in their pockets, "self-denial" was important in "the battle for a future not only secure, but full of the good things of life."

There was a striking similarity between the rhetoric of these advertisements and the content of stories featuring DC's two most popular characters, Superman and Batman. General works on American society between 1941 and 1945 and internal histories of the comic book industry note that comic book superheroes and publishers contributed to the war effort. But these accounts only touch on the sale of war bonds and the superpatriotism of some superheroes, such as Timely's Captain America; they do not consider the content of Superman and Batman stories. Superman and Batman stories often stood in marked contrast to the covers of DC's comic books. In addition to their war bonds covers, DC published a large number of battle action covers and patriotic scenes. For instance, between May 1942 and April 1943, eight of the twelve *Action Comics* covers dealt with the war. On the cover of the May 1942 issue, Superman fought a Japanese plane; on the November cover he opposed a German submarine. Superman also appeared with the U.S. flag on the cover of two issues of *Superman*. DC's covers gave the superheroes a military tone, but this characterization was largely symbolic and set off by the stories inside, which were about civilian life. Throughout the war DC published only one story in which Superman battled enemy armed forces, and even this occurred on American soil. Except for an explanatory note in *Superman*, no. 25 (November–December 1943), DC avoided the issue of Superman's service. But in mid-February 1942 the comic strip version of Superman had Clark Kent fail his physical by accidentally using his X-ray vision to read the eye chart in the next office. Shortly after, on March 11, Superman told the U.S. Congress that "the American armed forces are powerful enough to smash their treacherous foes without the aid of Superman." DC kept Superman out of the war because there was no way to explain why someone with his powers could not put an end to it.

Batman also stayed out of uniform, although he offered no excuse for his failure to join the armed services. Unlike Superman, and most other costumed heroes, Batman had no super powers. Batman was the secret identity of the playboy industrialist Bruce Wayne, who as a child had witnessed the murder of both his parents. Wayne then devoted his life to fighting crime and trained his body and mind for the task. If there was anything super about Batman, it was his psychotic drive to destroy criminals. Batman stories implied that he, as did Superman, believed the American people, empowered by democracy, needed no help from him on the battlefront to defeat fascism. Both characters dealt with fascist spies and saboteurs, and both *Batman* and *Superman* comic books ran stories about military training and on the need for greater public cooperation with the government's war effort. These stories stressed that "America's secret weapon [lay in] the courage of the common soldier" and that the war amounted to "Your Battle, Your Future, Your America!!!"

But DC published fewer than 15 of these stories among the over 500 Superman and Batman stories that appeared during the war. Most of these stories featured villains and criminals and had little military content. The powers and established characters of Superman and Batman probably limited DC's options for involving the two heroes in the war effort. But these limitations proved fortuitous as the company aligned the characters with home front campaigns for responsible consumption—an alignment that led to Superman's identification with the American way.

Parables of Consumption

The majority of war-era Superman and Batman stories depicted a universe in which American soldiers fought to establish world peace while the two superheroes helped to maintain a domestic order that supported the country's military endeavors. Most stories showed an American society relatively free from war-related strife and shortages but plagued by mad scientists, supervillains, and common criminals. Although the comic books encouraged the purchase of war bonds and supported paper, rubber, and metal salvage drives, writers and artists continued to present the United States as a consumer society with a bright future.

Consumption was not an explicit theme. Rather it formed the social backdrop in which stories were set. DC's writers and artists used Superman and Batman in stories about seemly manners of consumption in a war economy. Sometimes the company published comic book covers that affirmed consumption as a way of life. For instance, the November–December 1942 cover of *Superman* showed him carrying a car in which a family had all the accoutrements of a picnic. The comic appeared at the time of national concern over the shortage of rubber, and the cover showed tireless wheels. Amid the war-related covers of most of DC's comic books in 1942–43, this illustration attests to the validity and continuity of the family's way of life, even under war conditions. The cover was a celebration of ordinary American life enjoyed by the children and older folk pictured in the car and defended by men of service age, absent from the illustration. Life went on despite the absence of tires, sons, and fathers. The concurrent absence of servicemen and tires suggested that the two would return together.

Unlike war themes, which DC limited to covers and "Supermen of America" pages, writers created parables of consumption for Superman and Batman tales. Most Batman stories counterposed criminal consumer desire with virtuous acquisition of commodities through work. Batman dealt with a series of foes obsessed with acquiring gems and other high-priced gewgaws. Many Batman stories began with full-page surrealistic representations of these commodities, which suggested that it was an unreal desire for extravagant wealth that motivated criminals. Batman, who was in fact a millionaire, eschewed such wealth except insofar as it enabled him to combat crime. More important, he instilled the values of hard work and responsible consumption in his ward, Dick Grayson, who as Robin fought criminals alongside Batman. In a 1944 story Bruce Wayne puzzled over Dick's frequent absences from the house, only to discover that he had taken a job as a telegram boy to raise money for a birthday present because he had spent all his allowance on war bonds.

Superman combated a somewhat more powerful group of criminals and mad scientists than Batman did. But in general the plots of stories featuring the characters were much the same. In a May 1942 story Superman confronted a group of secondhand car dealers who, in search of quick profits and under the influence of a mysterious figure known as the Top, sold faulty vehicles. Confronted by mounting accidents and bad publicity, most of the dealers sought to reorganize their businesses and run them legitimately. They were able to do so when Superman broke up the Top's criminal organization. The story associated criminal activities with illicit business practices. It also linked legitimate business practices, in this case the fair trade of commodities in the market, with patriotism as the dealers, "freed from the Top's evil influence, . . . donated their imperfect cars" to the government's scrap metal drive for national defense.

"The Million-Dollar Marathon"

One Superman tale, "The Million-Dollar Marathon," stands out from other comic book stories as a commentary on appropriate and responsible consumption under wartime conditions. The story centered on Roger Treadwell's attempt to spend a million dollars in twenty-four hours so that he might inherit a larger sum.

Treadwell, a research physician at a children's hospital, planned to give his inheritance to the hospital but faced "the most perplexing problem he [had] ever encountered" in determining how to dispose of the initial million dollars, which he had to spend in single purchases of a thousand dollars each. His only idea was to buy a thousand dollars' worth of war bonds. With Lois Lane's help, he summoned Superman, who informed Treadwell, "It's a lot of money and you mustn't waste it . . . even though you can't give it away you'll have to spend it where it will do good." Superman then proceeded to buy laboratory supplies, save a mortgage that was about to be foreclosed, underwrite small businesses, and bid on art treasures at a sale to aid servicemen's families. In his most ambitious project Superman bought the material to construct a ship for an expedition in search of rare plants that would provide drugs to cure sick children. He even persuaded the government bureaucrat in charge of wartime resource allocation of the ship's importance to the war goal of caring for children, America's "best safeguard for the future." With Superman's aid Treadwell met the requirements of his inheritance, and all monies went to the children's hospital.

"The Million-Dollar Marathon" recast familiar tales about the dangers of unrestricted consumption as a parable of responsible wartime expenditure. But it was hardly a criticism of consumption as such. Approximating the numerous versions of *Brewster's Millions* and "Polly and Her Pals," the Superman story figured consumption as a test of virtue while inviting readers to enjoy vicariously its pleasures. The story's prologue informed readers that they would be "excited . . . over this amazing story of a man who wanted . . . to get rid of that magnificent sum, all within twenty-four hours! And if you think it's easy to spend and keep on spending, $41,666 an hour, nearly $695 a minute, you'll get a new slant on high finances as you watch Superman."

Other Superman tales also depicted a highly commodified society. For instance, in a 1943 story Lois Lane obtains a mink coat and goes on a shopping spree for accessories in six department stores, all of which are abundantly stocked. In 1944 DC prepared a special Superman comic book as a Christmas promotion for Bailey's department stores in Cleveland. The message of this twenty-page book was that American servicemen fought the war to ensure the right to celebrate Christmas. The accompanying advertising copy made it clear that Americans observed Christmas by purchasing and distributing large numbers of gifts, preferably from a Bailey's store. Shortly before the war's end a *Superman* cover depicted a domestic scene complete with refrigerator, anticipating a postwar America with a plentiful supply of consumer goods.

Ensuring a Prosperous Future

Comic books were advertisements that tied the promise of a society abundant in consumer goods to the defense of the nation. But they were also commodities themselves. Between 1941 and 1945 American servicemen purchased more of these commodities than any other reading material. The Second World War helped make comic books and the most popular superheroes, such as Superman, American institutions. Sales of comic books expanded to 60 million copies a month in 1947. The Superman/DC line of comic books was the most popular, selling an average of 8,500,000 copies a month in that year. DC expanded their marketing of Superman as a product. For instance, in the late 1940s the company licensed Superman movie serials and a television show that promoted him as a hero who fought for "Truth, Justice, and the American Way." DC also protected their market by suing the publishers of another comic book superhero, Captain Marvel, for copyright infringement. The success of this case removed Superman's major competitor and ensured DC dominance of the comic book field throughout the 1950s.

Comic book publishers, particularly DC, bound the war effort, democracy, consumer culture, and their superheroes together in the comic book and sold the total package as a commodity. Comic books illustrate the close connection in American society of democratic ideals and consumer culture. Superheroes' promotion of the war effort by upholding American values, such as the sanctity of private property and the pleasure of shopping, and the consumption of those heroes through comic books, demonstrate how corporate America has defined democracy in terms of the consumption of commodities. So successful were Superman and comic art in promoting the American way that even relatively militant unions produced comic book stories about democracy and consumption. In 1944 the Congress of Industrial Organizations (CIO) published a million copies of a comic-book-format pamphlet, *With Victory*, that looked forward to a richly commodified postwar America provided workers organized and voted to ensure the government took appropriate action. According to this comic, every soldier at the front dreamed of "a good job, a good wife, a good car, and some good kids." Reading comic books was one way soldiers sustained that dream throughout the war.

Battling the Red Menace in the Postwar Years

William W. Savage Jr.

After helping defeat the Axis forces in World War II, superheroes in the postwar years were enlisted to face a new threat to the American way of life—communism. Initially the scheming Russians—wartime allies of the United States—were the major antagonists to democratic ideals. As University of Oklahoma history professor William W. Savage Jr. explains in the following viewpoint, the line separating the ideologies of the United States and the Soviet Union was clearly drawn by 1947, and as a new cold war set in between the two countries, there were rampant fears that America was subject to infiltrators and fifth column subversives whose aim was to crush democracy and supplant it with totalitarian socialism. Comic-book writers latched on to those fears and pitted their superheroes and ace detectives against Communist agents who were out to steal U.S. technology—especially atomic secrets.

Savage concludes that comic-book artists over-simplified complex international events in an attempt to depict obvious heroes and villians. The battle lines in the pages of the comics were black and white, and American wisdom, talent, and values always proved superior to the Red Menace. Yet in the real world, the Cold War conflict was less clearly defined. China's embrace of communism and the fall of other

■

Southeast Asian nations to socialist revolutions suggested that communism's appeal was growing. And once the United States became involved in the civil war in Korea—a contest that was poorly managed and eventually fought to a draw—Americans began to question the costs of fighting to maintain democracy in nations halfway around the world.

THE STRUCTURE OF *STORY*, REGARDLESS OF THE medium through which it is told, requires some sort of conflict, and conflict requires some sort of resolution. As a matter of convenience, a reliable enemy is a fine thing for a storyteller to have. Artists, writers, and editors who earned their livings in the comic-book industry thus possessed ample reason to mourn the passing of the Axis leaders and their minions, having nothing handy to take their place except homegrown villains of the prewar years who were mild characters by comparison. Their criminal activities suggested nothing grand, no issue to inflame the imagination, nothing worth getting all stirred up about.

Some comic-book publishers tried to add zest by resurrecting the Third Reich—or was it the Fourth?—anticipating by at least three decades the preoccupation of other media with freeze-dried Nazis and Dr. Mengele's boys from Brazil [Hitler clones]. This was not the stuff of editorial backlog from the war years. Rather, it was material consciously generated to maintain a viable enemy at center stage, to keep a real war going, to blow a bit upon the patriotic spark. Was Hitler alive and well, hatching plans for world conquest from an underground city beneath Yellowstone National Park? Was the question worth asking, even in a comic book? One imagines public apathy reaching monumental proportions. Clearly, new kinds of enemies were needed—enemies mysterious and menacing, and whose appearance on the scene conveyed some sense of urgency to consumers of popular culture. In other words, the public deserved the sort of lasting malevolence to which it had become accustomed during World War II.

And then came the Communists, who seemed to fill the bill rather nicely from a storyteller's standpoint. They might not have been enlisted except for their own efforts, which, by 1947, were prodigious and thus worthy of extensive reportage. The relevant chronology included the enunciation of the Truman Doctrine aligning the United States against Communist terrorism in Turkey and Greece in the spring of 1947; the Soviet blockade of Berlin in the spring of 1948; the creation of NATO in August of 1949 to curb Russian expansionism; the severing of relations with Communist China in January 1950; and the commitment of American troops to Korea in June 1950. The Alger Hiss case, beginning late in 1948, the conviction in New York in October 1949 of eleven leaders of the American Communist Party for advocating the violent overthrow of the United States, and the trial of Julius and Ethel Rosenberg and Morton Sobell early in 1951 (we were missing a Bomb, remember) suggested the domestic aspect of international politics; and comic-book publishers had a Red Menace upon which to base their stories.

The principal villains had to be the Russians, since they seemed particularly determined to be difficult. They had come to think of the destruction of Nazi Germany as the occasion for helping themselves to half of Europe. Joseph Stalin was, by most accounts, not a nice man. The Soviets had shown an inordinate interest in our atomic secrets, had tried hard to filch them, and had succeeded, with an operational Bomb of their own by 1949. We had to be alert to the possibilities of a fifth column. Red infiltrators could be anywhere. Anyone inclined to relax in the midst of these prospects had only to await the morning newspaper and the next screaming headline. Popular wisdom had it that the United States should have allowed [General George S.] Patton's armor to keep on rolling, through Germany and into Russia. Then the world would not have been locked in its current sorry condition. And so forth.

Into the 1950s, the daily news confirmed everyone's worst suspicions. In Korea, Russia's Red Chinese stooges revealed the brutality of which the Communist nations were capable. In Washington, Harry Truman seemed to have misplaced his spine on the question of vaporizing evil people with tidbits from our atomic arsenal, even though he had sufficient backbone for dealing with the policy-making aspirations of General Douglas MacArthur. Better to elect a general to the presidency outright, people said—and better a general like Dwight Eisenhower than the egghead offered by the Democrats in 1952, even though Ike was the one who stopped Patton. And if the fires of hysteria did not burn as brightly as they had during the Red Scare of the 1920s, they were fanned periodically by ambitious politicians who understood that virulent anti-Communism was a good platform from which to publicize themselves. What Texas congressman Martin Dies had begun with the House Committee on Un-American Activities in the 1930s emerged full-blown (if not grown) in the 1950s as the national spotlight focused on the likes of Wisconsin Senator Joseph McCarthy and Californian Richard Nixon, soon to be the general's vice-president. It was a time of seemingly rampant anti-intellectualism, perfectly suited, the cynic might say, to the expounding of comic-book philosophies.

Scary Movies

In keeping with their performance during World War II, popular media tried—though not always successfully . . . —to respond in positive, supportive fashion. Hollywood, itself under considerable fire for harboring writers, directors, and actors who were, if not bright Red, then at least shockingly pink, tended to exploit paranoia to pack 'em in at the box office. Its films depicted constant, unrelieved menace from enemies so anonymous that they could be the lady in the supermarket or the neighbor down the street. Fighting ubiquitous evil was no simple matter, such films as *I Was a Communist for the FBI* (1951) and *Big Jim McLain* (1952) seemed to suggest; and if movies of that ilk were not enough to keep the average American looking over his or her shoulder and into other people's business, the ones that delighted in revealing national vulnerability certainly were. These were allegorical treatments from the genre of science fiction (or maybe horror), wherein aliens from Mars or elsewhere were employed to represent the Red Menace. Cold, calculating, and utterly incapable of emotion (thus conforming nicely to popular ideas of what godless Commies were all about), these creatures were doubly dangerous: Not only did they argue for a mindless communalism too horrible to contemplate, they also were either (1) extremely difficult to kill with conventional weapons, or (2) extremely

difficult to sort out of the general population, given their remarkable ability to look just like us. *The Thing from Another
World* (1951) and *Invasion of the Body Snatchers* (1956) were
prominent examples of Hollywood anti-Communism in the
alien-invader, we'll-all-be-zombies mode.

The Comics' Postwar Pragmatism

Comic books were considerably more optimistic, consistently
assuming the swift and inevitable downfall of all Communist
states, cells, and individuals. No need for paranoia from the
comic-book perspective, given the legion of federal agents on
the job to make the world safe for the American way. Comic
books baldly stated that *our* people, being bigger, smarter, and
tougher to start with, subdued *their* people every time. At
some point in virtually every story, American protagonists
took to muttering the sort of hard-boiled political preach-
ments that might have come from characters by Dashiell
Hammett or Raymond Chandler, had they been counterspies
instead of mere private detectives.

In touting the heroics of Treasury Department agents,
F.B.I. men, and operatives from various unnamed branches of
government, comic books indicated acceptance of, and appre-
ciation for, what might be called postwar pragmatism in dealing with Communists. American heroes, it seemed, were no
longer required to play fair with their enemies. Rather, they
fought fire with fire, in recognition of the dire consequences
awaiting the free world if they should fail in any of their respective missions. Merely neutralizing Soviet agents—or, for
that matter, Soviet armies—served no good purpose, given the
stakes in the game; so homicide, and not infrequently geno-
cide, became reasonable and acceptable undertakings for
comic-book operatives. It all reflected a redefinition of societal standards, dating, no doubt, from the adoption by the
United States of its enemies' tactics during World War II—
. . . [the] bombing of civilian populations. A nation that will assert the righteousness of its cause through those means can ill-
afford to employ agents unprepared to acknowledge the effi-
caciousness of such approaches—or to employ them, should
push come to shove. Theirs was not to reason why, simply because there was no need for intellectual rumination. And, sane

people that they were, comic-book secret agents knew that it was better to kill a few Soviets, or a few hundred, or a few thousand, than to risk having Europe and the Americas over-run by Communist forces. Presumably, it was also better than having to kill a few million Russians in an atomic war, although comic-book writers did not expound that philosophy in any certain terms. . . .

Good Russians, Bad Russians

If, on the one hand, comic books relied upon the implacable enmity of the Soviet regime in the early 1950s, they did, on the other hand, differentiate between the Russian people and their leaders. Here was a new courtesy, one scarcely extended to the German or Japanese populations during World War II. Russia had been an ally in the fight against Hitler, at least up to a point. Some comic books had gone so far as to lionize the Russian fighting man and woman, establishing them as worthy companions to the American soldier, and, on occasion, even as sidekicks. Without that background, however, sympathy for the average Russian was still possible, owing to the prevalent perception of Communism as a political deal. According to the comic-book argument, the Russian Revolution had been a good and necessary thing, a movement of and by the people to liberate themselves from the yoke of Tsarist oppression. It may even have been comparable to the American Revolution in that regard. But, unhappily for the Russian people, their revolution was appropriated by a cruel, heartless group bent on the creation of a totalitarian state and capable, as it turned out, of violent excess far beyond any that the Tsar and his followers might have imagined. Thus, an otherwise virtuous revolution had resulted in the creation of a true police state and the emergence of Stalin's monstrous dictatorship; and the Russian people were, by the early 1950s, worse off than they had ever been before. As American comic books had it, Russia was a place where heavily armed soldiers waited in the underbrush to machine-gun hardworking peasants who dared to relate this forbidden history to their innocent children.

American comic books interpreted the Chinese revolutionary experience in a somewhat different light. Dr. Sun Yat-sen, the revolutionary democratic nationalist, was the early hero; but he made the mistake of agreeing to accept Communist aid, and that brought in the Soviets, and there went the revolution—another popular movement usurped by the powers of political darkness. Hope for the future of a democratic China lay with Chiang Kai-shek's army on Formosa and its continuing efforts, with American support, to overthrow the Communists occupying the mainland.

Oversimplifying a Complex Issue

Such interpretations indicated that comic books were trying harder than ever before to inform American readers about the origins of current problems. One might easily debate the question of whether the data were intended to educate or to indoctrinate, but the significant point is that the data appeared at all. Here were explanations of world crisis a good deal more complex than those offered during World War II, perhaps reflecting the public perception that the world itself was a good deal more complex than it had been before 1945. Still, for all their weaving of tales about good revolutions subverted by bad people, comic books oversimplified for the sake of the argument no less than for the preferences of the market. Comic-book interpretations ignored vast swatches of inconvenient history, so that one did not have to consider, say, Chiang Kai-shek's education in Moscow and his massacres of Communist workers in northern China in the 1920s in juxtaposition to his status as democracy's Asiatic spokesman in the 1950s.

Inherent in the comic-book perspective on the Communist world was the notion that the enslaved masses of Russia, China, and assorted satellites ached to recapture their respective revolutions and cast out the agents of Soviet tyranny as the first order of business. Practically, such thinking tended to lower the odds against the comic-book spies and counterspies in the employ of the United States, indicating to the truly concerned reader that all a fellow really had to do was topple one or two members of the inner circle. Then, because one thing leads to another (as in the case of falling dominoes), the whole Communist bloc would crumble. Comic-book agents were not superheroes, and this sort of convention gave American protagonists an edge. It suggested that, at least on one level, the Cold War was a better conflict than World War II had been, to the extent that America's enemies were not fanatical populations but merely a few hundred fanatical individuals. It also suggested that most of the nations of the world could elude the Red Menace with just a little help from their American friends.

Cool, Efficient American Agents

Because American comic-book agents worked alone or in pairs —seldom were more than two ever required to thwart any Communist plot—the "domino" convention served to indicate the fragile underpinning of each subversive enterprise. American agents always aimed for the top man; and when he fell, of course, the whole plot collapsed. In this way, comic books stressed the superiority of American intellect by demonstrating the inferiority of the Communist mind. No matter how complex the Communist plan, and regardless of the amount of effort put into it, the comic-book agent had only to locate the proper domino and push.

Consider the September 1951 issue of *Kent Blake of the Secret Service*, wherein the protagonist parachuted into Tibet to learn why the Dalai Lama had begun "preaching a holy war against the western hemisphere." In the bowels of the Pentagon, Agent Blake's boss had explained the urgency of the mission: "First there were stirrings of unrest. Now all of Asia is inflamed and awaiting his final word! If the Asiatic hordes are properly armed they could sweep over all of Asia, Europe, and Africa . . . then deal the death blow to our own civilization!"

Naturally, there had to be Communist influence behind anything as potentially devastating as that; and, sure enough, Blake learned that two Soviet agents had entered Tibet and murdered the Dalai Lama. One of them had assumed the holy man's identity and was in the process of inflaming the masses. Blake, alone and in unfamiliar territory, managed to expose the plot, kill the two Soviet spies, and install the dead Dalai Lama's brother as the new spiritual leader. The tale ended with all the customary platitudes: America's flag would fly "high and proud" as long as the nation continued to produce men like Agent Blake, etc., etc. But Blake, for his part, shrugged off the whole adventure and took a nap.

American agents were at home anywhere in the world, it seemed, and coolly efficient, whatever their surroundings and regardless of their circumstances. Few were as casual as the sleepy Kent Blake, however. Clark Mason, for example, was an antipodal character, tough to the point of ruthlessness, and an utterer, not of platitudes, but of tight-lipped eulogies delivered over the corpses of his Communist foes. Even the presence of his frequent companion, a fetching female spy known as Vicki, could not soften his visage or demeanor as he dealt death to America's enemies. Of course, Mason often confronted more complicated situations than agents like Blake did, and so he enjoyed a smaller margin of error and had less fun.

In the November 1951 issue of *Spy Fighters*, Mason and Vicki entered Albania with orders to prove that refugees supposedly fleeing from Yugoslavia were fictitious creations of Soviet anti-Tito propaganda. As it happened, the migration into Albania was genuine, but no refugees were crossing the border. Rather, the immigrants were Russian soldiers in mufti, assembling inside Albania and poised to strike at Europe. Mason foiled the plot by nailing the Russian officer in charge of the operation. The proper domino having been pushed, the entire plan failed, and the Russian was left to face music composed by his superiors at home. Spat Mason in conclusion, "There's only *one* refuge for a disgraced Commie! A little six by four territory where they *all* belong!"

A Difficult Time for Comics

Gutsy rhetoric aside, here were yarns with geo-political points of reference baffling to the adolescent and irrelevant to adults who read comic books for whatever visceral enjoyment might come from pictorial Red-bashing. *Foreign Affairs* it was not, but comic-book producers seemed to believe that the medium owed such accounts to its audience. The lengths to which artists and writers might go were suggested by a story concerning Communist activities in Kashmir in the April 1952 issue of *Spy Cases*. It featured a map and a two-page introduction to the history of Hindu-Moslem relations in the region, as well as background on the long-standing conflict between India and Pakistan, which, of course, the Soviets wished to exploit, since a full-blown war between those nations would pave the way for a Communist takeover. Then and only then came Doug Grant, comic-book secret agent, to resolve matters involving a wealthy rug-merchant's secretly Communist daughter, a kidnapped American girl, and a yogi who had sat in cross-legged meditation in the mountains of Kashmir for twenty years without so much as a word to anyone until, upon observing Grant's struggle against overwhelming Communist odds, he hopped up to announce, "I will not stand by and watch liberty destroyed," and proceeded to save the American's life. It wanted a [patriotic music composer John Philip] Sousa sound track and footnotes by [U.S. cold war diplomat] George F. Kennan to round out the high drama in mountainous places, but, alas, it was only a story in a comic book, no more or less absurd than any other of its kind.

And therein lay the rub: Communists were having an easy time in the world, it seemed; and, no matter how great the desire of foreign peoples for peace and freedom, it always took an American to promote change. Why were these people so completely unable to help themselves? They adored liberty, or so they said, and they outnumbered the Soviet agents who made their lives miserable. Why, then, could they not arise and slay the enemy as he slept? If comic books strived diligently for verisimilitude with maps and socio-political discourse, why was theirs a world so defiant of the logic inherent in the black-and-white values that had sustained the medium during World War II? Comic books appeared to have painted themselves into an unhappy corner with multiple shadings from a confused palette. They were too much of the world, and the world was no longer suited to the renditions of a popular art that had, for the moment, misplaced the lowest common denominator. Comic books may have invented the friendly Bomb, but clearly that was not enough.

There is a bad old joke about a chameleon who sat upon a patchwork quilt and experienced a nervous breakdown. From that imagery, however, one may discern the dilemma of the comic-book medium in post–World War II America. Comic books sought to mirror the real world for readers for whom mere escapism was no longer a satisfying indulgence. But the reflection they cast was disturbing in its implications and made escape seem somehow more desirable. Readers demanded a world they could understand, a world that corresponded to common sense. Thus, American spies like Clark Mason and

Doug Grant left Tibet and Albania and Kashmir and went in uniform to the battleground of Korea, to serve as military intelligence officers in a simpler, less ambiguous theater of operations, where black and white were once again the dominant colors. The ploy, however, resolved nothing except perhaps the publishers' problem: Korea, as it turned out, was not the stuff to salve the American psyche.

The Comics Code: Creators Agree to Self-Censor

Amy Kiste Nyberg

The Comics Code is a set of regulatory guidelines created and adopted by major publishers of comic books. The first code was established in 1954 following Senate subcommittee investigations into the possible ill effects of comic books on America's youth. The investigations were prompted by the work of Frederic Wertham, a psychiatrist whose book *Seduction of the Innocent* fingered comic books as one manifestation of society's love affair with violence and immorality that promoted juvenile delinquency and other childhood disorders. In the following article, Amy Kiste Nyberg, an assistant professor at Seton Hall University in New Jersey and the author of *Seal of Approval: The History of the Comics Code*, sketches the atmosphere of the postwar years that led to the implementation of regulations within the comics industry. She notes that, contrary to popular belief, comic-book publishers were by and large not affected by the code. The graphic horror comics of publisher William Gaines were the most notable casualty of the new regulations, but most major publishers contentedly obliged the concerned public and adhered to the concept of producing wholesome comics. Since its inception in the mid-1950s, the Comics Code has been amended and revised to suit the changing times. It is still in effect today.

■

THE COMICS CODE SEAL OF APPROVAL BEARS THE message "Approved by the comics code authority" and first appeared on the covers of comic books in the mid-1950s. The comics code is a set of regulatory guidelines primarily concerned with sex, violence, and language drawn up by publishers and enforced by the "code authority," a euphemism for the censor employed by the publishers. Comic books passing the prepublication review process are entitled to carry the seal of approval. This study of the origins and history of the comics code examines how and why such a code came into being and the code's significance both historically and to comic book publishing today. . . .

Controlling Children's Culture

To begin, it is important to recognize that the postwar comic book controversy has its roots in earlier attitudes toward comic books and toward popular culture more generally. Most of the investigations of the comics code to date have focused on criticisms of comic books in the postwar period, specifically 1948 to 1954, but by limiting their study to this time frame, researchers have failed to recognize important links between the campaign against comic books and previous efforts to control children's culture. Far from being an isolated instance of Cold War hysteria, the debate over comic books fits into a broad pattern of efforts to control children's culture. As film, radio, and comic books each were introduced and became part of children's leisure activities, guardians of children's morality renewed their attacks on the mass media.

From the outset, symbols of social authority over childhood and children's reading, particularly teachers and librarians, defined comic book reading as a problem. They expressed fears that the comic book was leading children away from better literature and creating a generation of semi-literates. When academic researchers began to test some of the assumptions educators were making about comic books, however, their findings demonstrated that comic book reading made little difference in the acquisition of reading skills, in academic achievement, or in social adjustment. Despite these research findings, the criticism of comic books persisted because the fears about comic books, rather than being based on empirical evidence, were rooted in adult beliefs and attitudes about children's leisure time activities. Adults' concern stemmed in large part from fears that children's culture, especially the control of leisure reading, had escaped traditional authority. Adults believed that children's free time should be spent in constructive activities that would improve their mental and physical well-being, failing to understand the appeal of comic books, which they perceived as simplistic, crude, and lacking artistic or literary merit. Reading comic books was, plain and simple, a waste of time and money. The struggle between children's taste and adult authority was presented as a "challenge" to be faced and a "battle" to be won; adults sought to substitute their own choices for the comic books favored by children.

Link to Juvenile Delinquency

Alarm over this contamination of children's culture failed to produce a sustained public reaction. Evidence suggests that the "problem" of comic books entered public discourse only after those seeking to control children's culture, allied with church and civic groups that traditionally enforced standards of public morality, were able to gain the attention of the popular press. The major factor in the success of the campaign against comics was the linkage of comic book reading to juvenile delinquency, a problem representing the ultimate loss of social control over children. When the antecedents of the postwar campaign against comics are understood, it becomes clear that while the debate shifted from an emphasis on education and morality to one of law and order, the fundamental concern—social control of children—remained the same. The impetus for the shift in the debate was the emergence of experts such as psychiatrist Fredric Wertham [author of *Seduction of the Innocent*] whose crusade against comics was a significant factor in focusing public attention on the medium and in legitimating the views of those who saw comic books as a threat to children. . . .

At the local level, civic and religious groups acted to impose standards on comic books and brought pressure to bear on the retailers in their communities. These groups, which had no legal power, used the economic threat of boycotts to force retailers to remove from their shelves comic books deemed unsuitable. Such decency crusades were aided by ratings lists published by the Catholic Church's National Office of Decent Literature and by the Cincinnati Committee for the Evaluation of Comics, whose lists were published in *Parents' Magazine.* These efforts attracted the attention of lawmakers at the state and national level. In the years following World War II, several states appointed legislative committees to study the problem and recommend laws aimed at curbing undesirable comic books. At the national level, the Investigation of comic books was carried out by the Senate Subcommittee to Investigate Juvenile Delinquency, which undertook a study of the relationship of the mass media to the problem of delinquency.

The key witness at the Senate hearings and the leader of the crusade against comics was Wertham. He took the position that comic books were harmful, and he pressed for legislation

A Chilling Effect on the Comic Book Industry

With publication of the March 1955 issues, almost all major publishers had the Comics Code Authority "seal of approval" emblazoned on the covers of their comic books. Many scrambled to make the last-minute changes in their books that the new Code required. Artists frantically inked over plunging cleavage and erased away blazing guns so that stories already produced could be published under the new Code restrictions.

William Gaines at EC Comics responded to the new Code by replacing his horror comics with titles like *Psychoanalysis*, *Extra*, and *Impact*. These "New Direction" comics dealt with material that fell within the Code's guidelines, but distribution problems would kill off the entire EC comic-book line within the year.

Stanley P. Morse, another publisher who had depended heavily upon horror comics, shut down all four of his comic-book publishing companies. Star Publications, restricting the sale of comic books to children under age sixteen. But Wertham's argument was much more complex than the idea he was often accused of perpetrating: that there was a direct causal link between comic book reading and juvenile delinquency. The problem of juvenile delinquency, he believed, stemmed from the fact that society was trapped in a "cult of violence" of which comic books were simply a manifestation. While he acknowledged that eliminating harmful comic books would not solve the problem of juvenile delinquency, he was convinced that such action would be a step in the right direction.

Many media scholars have dismissed Wertham's work as an example of early, unsophisticated social science research into media effects, and contemporary social scientists criticized Wertham for his lack of scientific methodology and his

Sterling Comics, Toby Press, United Feature, and Eastern Color also went out of business this year. While most of the failed publishers were somewhat small, both United and Eastern had been successful in the field since its inception. . . .

Dell Comics, perhaps the publisher least affected by the Comics Code, was prospering. Its chief mainstays of funny-animal and western comics were ideally suited to the times, and readership remained fairly steady.

For the most part, however, the Code seemed to have had a chilling effect on the comic-book industry. Although publishers brought out more romance, western, and humor comics to replace their horror and crime comics, the overall effect was a big drop in the number of titles.

From an all-time industry high of six hundred fifty titles in 1954, there were now barely more than three hundred titles—a fifty percent-plus drop. Artists and writers left the field, publishers closed their doors, and circulation fell.

Mike Benton, *The Comic Book in America: An Illustrated History.* Dallas: Taylor, 1989, pp. 53–55.

failure to present quantitative evidence to support his findings. I argue, however, that the image of Wertham as a misguided pioneer in media effects research is erroneous. In fact, Wertham attacked the emerging social science approach to media effects research, calling instead for a multidisciplinary study of mass media. He believed his approach, which he called the clinical method, with its detailed case histories, observation, and follow-up, was the only valid way to study long-term media effects.

Adopting a Comics Code

Despite Wertham's efforts, the Senate subcommittee failed to recommend any legislative remedy for the problem of comic books, instead calling on the industry to police itself. The passage of the comics code in October 1954 pacified many of the groups calling for censorship and put to rest any fears that the industry would be regulated by the government. The models for self-regulation of the comic book industry were the codes adopted by other mass media. Since many of the criticisms of film were repeated almost verbatim about comic books, the film industry provided a compatible model for comics publishers, and the comics code is nothing more than a rewrite of the Film Production Code of the 1930s. The bulk of the comics code dealt with crime and horror, the two topics that had brought public ire down on the heads of publishers. The code continued to allow publication of crime comics within new, strict guidelines but banned publication of horror comics. But publishers went beyond the criticisms voiced against comics to address the complaints of groups more concerned with morality than delinquency, adding provisions dealing with language, costume, and the portrayal of family values, following the lead of the Film Production Code in these areas.

There is a persistent belief among the fan-historians that the comic book industry was nearly destroyed by the comics code, a view accepted by academic researchers. Such a view ignores other, more important influences. While the years following the adoption of the code were a period of upheaval in the industry, the implementation of the comics code was only part of the explanation for the industry's difficulties. First, the distribution problems the industry experienced in the mid-

1950s were due not to retailers' resistance to carrying the "controversial" comics but rather to the decision by American News Company, which distributed more than half of all comic books published at the time, to pull out of magazine distribution following federal antitrust action. The demise of American News Company left many publishers without a way to distribute their titles. Second, many of the companies that went out of business were simply victims of a more general economic hardship brought about by the drop in sales of comic books. This decrease was attributable to two factors. One was negative publicity about comic books, but a second factor was the increasing competition from television for children's leisure time. James Baughman, in his analysis of the impact of television on mass media industries in postwar America, has suggested that the introduction of television marginalized other mass media, forcing them increasingly to compete for a share of the audience's time that was not being spent watching television. Although Baughman does not address comic books specifically, it is clear from his analysis that the failure of comic books to regain their status as a mass medium can be linked to much broader trends in all media industries. The scramble by comic book publishers to reestablish themselves in the marketplace was mirrored by similar efforts among newspaper publishers, magazine publishers, film companies, and radio networks.

Effects of the Code

It is true that some companies, such as William Gaines's E.C. Comics, were casualties of the new standards; in fact, most fan-historians focus on the demise of E.C. Comics as an example of the impact of the code. But what happened to Gaines was the exception rather than the rule. Many publishers continued to add new titles, and by the end of the decade, with the reintroduction of the superheroes who would launch the "Silver Age" of comics, the comic book industry regained some of the ground it had lost a few years earlier. Gaines's comic books from that period have been reprinted for new generations of fans, and today E.C. Comics are recognized as a significant contribution both for their artwork and their storytelling. If there is a "canon" of comic books, E.C. Comics may be found at the head of the list. This reverence for E.C. Comics of the 1950s helps to explain why the demise of Gaines's company is equated to the destruction of an entire industry in that period. It is important to separate the impact of the code on the creative output of the industry from its impact on comic book publishing. While one may argue that the comics code harmed the creative development of comic books, it is much more difficult to support the argument that the comics code almost destroyed the comic book publishing industry.

Gaines was not the only publisher unhappy with the code. Those who sat on the executive board of the Comics Magazine Association of America, the trade organization formed and supported by the publishers to administer the code, would debate the provisions and the very need for a code at almost every meeting. Changes were made to the code in 1971 and again in 1989. In 1971, changing social values, the emergence of underground "comix," and a depressed market combined to force the publishers into relaxing some of the restrictions on comic book content to allow publishers to bring their comics more in line with contemporary standards. Regulations on both the depiction of sex and violence were rewritten, and a section on how to show drug use and abuse was added. But the four publishers who remained active in the Comics Magazine Association of America during the late 1970s and the 1980s—Archie, Marvel, Harvey, and DC—continued to challenge the need for a code. The next change to the code, enacted in 1989, was due in large part to changes in comic book distribution and audience demographics and to competition from a new group of "independent" comic book publishers. Instead of selling comics only through the magazine distribution system, publishers began, in the 1970s, to market comic books through a new network of distributors and retailers developed exclusively for comic books. In addition, the audience for comic books, rather than being the preteens of the 1940s and 1950s, was more likely to be older teens or young adults. And finally, a number of upstart companies began to publish comics that were more experimental and adult in their themes. The 1989 code eliminated the detailed lists of what was forbidden, instead offering a more general set of "principles" in various categories. A second portion of the code, not intended for public distribution, gave more specific editorial guidelines to publishers, editors, and artists. Despite the seeming flexibility built into the 1989 version of the code, it is still clearly the intention of the comic book publishing industry that comic books carrying the code seal of approval be appropriate for children of all ages.

Underground Comix and the 1960s Counterculture

Patrick Rosenkranz

The counterculture of the 1960s thrived on artistic freedom. One avenue of expression was a reinvention of the comic book. Mainstream comics had always dealt with mainly juvenile audiences, and their world-view either embraced the status quo or wavered into superpatriotism. Bored with the conventions and bland content of these publications, visionary counterculture artists and writers began creating small press comics that dealt with drugs, free love, the Vietnam War, and a host of other antiestablishment topics. By 1968, many of these artists converged on San Francisco, the nucleus of the counterculture movement. There, a small collective produced *Zap Comics*, the earliest and most influential of the new breed. The first issue of *Zap Comics* was the work of Robert Crumb, one of the founders of the underground art scene. Crumb drew stories of middle-class paranoiacs, sexual deviates, drug trippers, and self-righteous idiots. The art seemed to blur the line between social satire and obscenity, and because of that, *Zap* began selling.

Zap Comics inspired imitation, and soon several underground presses such as Print Mint, Rip Off Press, and Apex Novelties were cranking out hundreds

■

of homemade comics—or "underground comix" as they were called to distinguish them from the mainstream publications. In the following selection from his history of underground comix, Patrick Rosenkranz provides glimpses of the movement as it blossomed in 1969. Rosenkranz reveals that the underground scene was home to many talented artists who knew of or worked with each other. They pursued their craft tirelessly, overcoming financial difficulties, obstinate printers, police raids, and natural disasters to publish even small quantities of their work. The notoriety of underground comix kept the movement alive into the 1970s. After that, much of what was once underground became accepted into and even co-opted by mainstream society. Patrick Rosenkranz is an author, filmmaker, and photojournalist who has written extensively on underground art since 1969.

THE RAPID SUCCESS OF *ZAP COMICS* BROUGHT new talent to San Francisco in a hurry. Most of the cartoonists working for East Coast underground newspapers packed up their meager possessions and moved west. By 1969, the core group that would define underground comix was assembled in the City by the Bay. *Zap* was a closed shop by then, so newcomers had to create their own comic titles. Unlike the overground market, which produced continuing comic titles on a regular schedule, the undergrounders came up with new titles all the time, and deadlines were a more casual affair. The booming counterculture population embraced comix enthusiastically, and many titles became big sellers, crunching the kinds of numbers that Marvel and DC were used to. Sales of the *Zaps* steadily climbed to the one million mark by the early 1970s.

In this optimistic atmosphere, anything seemed possible. . . .

Looking for Work

In 1969 [Philadelphia artist] Greg Irons moved back to San Francisco, and found that time had not stood still. A new scene was happening, and poster work was harder to find. . . .

Irons soon realized that comix were hot and posters were

not. He went to see Rick Griffin, who was still designing posters, but was also doing pages for *Zap Comics*. "It was his transition from posters to comics that made me think about doing it," said Irons. "I drew a hundred pages of comics when I was in the sixth grade, you know. So comics weren't something that was new to me, but underground comics were because they were just a new phenomena."

Griffin encouraged Irons to draw something for *Zap*, who drew some pages and took them to Robert Crumb. "Crumb was real positive," recalled Irons. "He said, 'This stuff doesn't look real finished.' And I looked at it and it wasn't. It was done on notebook paper; it was real shaky stuff, you know?" Irons redrew the story and brought it back and gave it to Dana Crumb [the wife of Robert Crumb], but the strip got misplaced, he said. "I found myself not in *Zap*, and in fact with my art work lost. So I redid that comic strip and submitted it to the Schenkers at the Print Mint who were publishing *Yellow Dog* and they published it," said Irons. "Which was okay, I mean I didn't feel too left out about that because there were a lot of other people around who were in the same boat as me."

Irons decided to do a solo comic book to build his reputation and began work on what would become *Heavy Tragic-Comics*. In the meantime, he landed some paying work designing record albums and promotional materials for [rock bands] Blue Cheer and Cold Blood. . . .

In the summer of 1969, Dave Sheridan and Fred Schrier drove from Cleveland to San Francisco in Sheridan's Sprite, which they renamed the Overland Vegetable Stagecoach after they arrived, when they discovered some potatoes under the seat.

When they got to the Bay Area, they stopped in to see [comics artist Gilbert] Shelton and the crew at Rip Off Press. [Comics artist Jack] Jackson remembered looking at their portfolios. "I took a look at Sheridan's stuff and it really knocked me out," he said. "It was great stuff. Then Schrier showed his stuff and it was terrible. I kind of said, 'Sheridan, we'd love to publish your stuff, but I don't know about Schrier yet.' Sheridan said 'We only publish together.' We said OK, what the hell. Within a year, Schrier's style had developed to where it was almost better in some respects than Sheridan's.

You have to look at new material that's not so good and try to see the potential in it."

The Ohio duo was almost finished with the artwork for *Mother Oats Comix*, which was published by Rip Off Press late in 1969. They also produced work for a new anthology book, *Slow Death Funnies*, which was being published by Ron Turner of Last Gasp Eco-Funnies. "It was one of the two paying comic jobs around," said Sheridan. "He was soliciting and we were starving, so we did it. He was the only other thing going besides *Zap*."

Mother Oats Comix #1, which kicked off the amazing dope tales genre, was a hit with the hip crowd, so they started work on issue #2. *Mother Oats* introduced the quintessential marijuana merchant, Dealer McDope, who later became the poster boy for the California Marijuana Initiative and the subject of a board game designed by Tom Patchett and published by Last Gasp.

The Overland Vegetable Stagecoach team expanded to include several other friends working in Los Angeles and New York. Sheridan drew some counter-advertisements for a Washington, D.C. lobby called the Stern Concern, did record promotions, and other non-comic, rent-paying jobs. "The comix don't really support me. I couldn't live just on the money from comics." A home brew enthusiast, he designed a series of beer labels that later became t-shirt designs, including "Industrial Strength Malt Liquor" and "Black Death Malt Liquor." After *Mother Oats Comix* #2 was published, Schrier left California to join the Peace Corps and serve in Afghanistan. . . .

Inspiration into Action

Ron Turner worked part time at Kaiser Hospital in fall 1968, while he finished his graduate studies at San Francisco State. A co-worker, Keith Albert, invited him to a New Year's Eve party in Berkeley. "Everybody got pretty stoned and he brought out a copy of *Zap Comics* #1," recalled Turner. "It just blew my mind. I took it back to the bedroom and read it again and again. It was crazy. It really knocked my socks off. It had captured my attention as readily as comics had done as a kid and I liked that feeling, to be back that way, to be totally engrossed, to be completely captured by these images. So suddenly *Zap Comics* came into my life and everything changed."

The first thing he needed to do was find more of these comic books, he said. "It took a while but I located Gary Arlington. He would sell these things like *Snatch Comics*, from under the counter in his store. . . .

Rod Frieland, who worked as a printer at the Berkeley Ecology Center, suggested that Turner create an ecology comic book to benefit the center. "We all thought underground comix were the greatest thing in the world as far as a propaganda tool to pass information along," said Turner. "Not only were they funny and unique but they appealed universally to young people. If we could do a comic book on ecology this would be a great thing. At the same time, we could have a revenue source for the ecology center." Their next consideration was financing. "I found a guy who had an acid lab in Berkeley and he imported marijuana and he had extra money. He put money into the Ecology Center Bookstore and he was willing to lend me 2500 bucks or so for this project."

Gary Arlington introduced Turner to several underground cartoonists, starting with Greg Irons, who agreed to edit the first issue of *Slow Death Funnies* and to draw the cover, which showed a voracious monster devouring its own planet. "In a couple of months we pulled a comic book together, and had Don Donahue print the covers," said Turner. "So he locked himself in the *Good Times Commune* in the basement where the press was then with a couple of bottles for about a week and printed the damn things up." The inside newsprint pages had to be printed on a larger press, and their choices were limited. "Warren Wallet's Press and Howard Quinn were the two companies that would print the word 'f——'," said Turner. "That was the criteria in those days. You would ask the printer, do you have any objection to printing the word 'f——?' If the answer was no, you would do business with them, if their price was right.". . .

A few months later, Turner published his second title, *It Ain't Me Babe*, which featured the work of seven female artists. Before the year was out, he had also issued a second *Slow Death Funnies* and had taken over *Skull Comics* from Rip Off Press with issue #2. Rip Off and Print Mint offered to trade their comics for his, so Turner also found himself in the distribution business. "I started building up distribution. At one point I had 200 stores in the Bay Area that were on various routes." After a while his partner convinced Turner he was too valuable to be driving the truck and should be working in the office, and brought a friend in from New Mexico to take over the routes. Unfortunately, marijuana runs gradually replaced comic book distribution, said Turner. "Basically they turned it into a place to sell pounds up and down the hills and across the country."

A Surreal Scene

In 1969 Rip Off Press . . . moved into the top floor of Mowry's Opera House. "The deal at the time was that for $25 a month, you could get a key to the place and do whatever you wanted that the other key holders would allow you to get away with," said Fred Todd. "This was definitely a good location for underground comix." Jack Jackson later memorialized these times in his strip "Rip Off Press: The Golden Era," which appeared in *Rip Off Comix* #21 in 1989.

[An underground filmmaker also used Mowry's for his naked theater troupe.] Naked actresses often cavorted right next to their shop, said Todd, which confirmed his belief that operating heavy machinery in the presence of nudity was not a good idea, especially for longhaired printers. "I was going to the Art Institute at the time and was really desensitized to naked female flesh," claimed Todd. "I'd been drawing naked women all day, and when I came in there were naked women running around. Who cares? But [comics editor Dave] Moriarty was beside himself." Either gawk or run the press, but don't try to do both at once, they advised him, as they unwound his ponytail from the rollers. . . .

"For every good cover we got out of it, we got about ten trashed-out covers," said Jackson. "Finally after we had run enough to do the issue up, we started experimenting, and we started taking one plate off, say the blue plate, and running it in red. Just screwing around. We were just playing and having some fun in those days. It wasn't really that serious a deal.". . .

[After a fire at Mowry's the building owners insisted that Rip Off Press] move into a storefront in another of their buildings at the corner of Golden Gate and Franklin Street, which was the best site yet, said Todd. The rent was sixty dollars a month, but the city never came around to collect it. They put up a sign on the side of the building that said "Rip Off Press, Fine Pirnting" [sic]. Periodically someone would come by and tell them not to get too comfortable, because the building, a four-story hotel, was slated for destruction at some date in the near future. They were the only tenants in the whole place, and it seemed a shame to let all that empty space just sit there, they decided. "After we were there a while, we opened little holes into the other parts of the building and expanded—took over the hotel and had a bunch of people living there. It was a real circus," said Todd. . . .

Despite the distractions, the partners slowly became more competent printers. By this time they were doing about one third publishing and two-thirds job printing, Todd estimated. Their new comics included *Subvert* #1, *Motor City* #2, and *Exile into Consciousness*, and they printed several posters and t-shirts as well. All this merchandise sold fairly well, but the golden goose of their publishing line for the next decade turned out to be the amazing dope adventures of those three rascally radicals, the hippie stooges with hearts of Acapulco Gold, the Fabulous Furry Freak Brothers.

Crumb Retreats Inward

In 1969, Crumb resolved to make himself a moving target. "My pissant little fame had made my life so completely crazy by this time. I was only able to keep up the cartooning through sheer momentum. Most of my energy was now focused on dealing with the endless procession of hustlers and hangers-on, and getting rid of all this pent-up sex rage. The comics definitely suffered."

Some readers thought they improved. The characters were better developed and there was definitely a lot more kinky sex in them. It probably had something to do with all the women who wanted to bask in the aura of his fame. "How did I ever get any work done?" he wondered. "I look at all the comics I cranked out then and wonder how I did it. Plus, I was running all over the goddam country. Most of *Big Ass Comics* #1 was drawn in LA, *Motor City* #1 in Detroit. I spent time in Chicago, Milwaukee, New York. Fame opened doors for me everywhere! I could ease right into the local hippie scene in big college towns like Ann Arbor [Michigan] and Madison

[Wisconsin]. I drew comics in all these places, and met girls, and had loose sex. I got the clap. I got crabs. Lucky for our generation there was no AIDS yet."

The peace and love generation was splintering into feuding factions, and he soon realized that he couldn't please them all, not if he wanted to remain honest in his work. When he created *Motor City's* Lenore Goldberg many comics readers hailed her as a feminist role model because she espoused the tenets of the women's liberation movement. She was a smart, strong, take-charge woman with big boots and a bad attitude. However, Crumb's unabashed presentation of "weird sex fantasies with the behind in mind" in *Big Ass Comics* alienated a faction of his former fans. Eggs Ackley's domination and deflowering of leather clad vulture babes smacked of counterrevolutionary male oppression fantasies, according to some critics. Female comics readers preferred the cuter aspects of his early *Zap* characters, said Crumb. . . .

Crumb delved into murky personal regions, using the camouflage of comic books to examine his own subconscious. "One of the keys to expressing yourself in your art is to try to break through self-restraint, to see if you can get past that socialized part of your mind, the superego or whatever you call it," he insisted. "I know from my own work I have to let that stuff out, it can't stay inside of me: all the craziness, the sexual stuff, the hostility toward women, the anger toward authority. I've actually worked a lot of that out of my system in my work. In my early period I did a lot more violent, anti-authoritarian stuff than I do now. In this one story I had myself chopping this nun's head off. I had to do that, it had to come out." While some readers were appalled by these visions, his fellow artists and many fans loved the sexual iconoclasm of his new work. Prolific despite the distractions in his personal life, Crumb produced 160 published comic pages in 1969 and an equal number in 1970. . . .

Zap Gets Zapped

The best-selling title in the underground was still *Zap Comics*, which became the standard bearer for quality and content. As each new issue appeared, the Zapsters strove to outdo themselves, to broach new subjects and styles, and to create new art with the hybrid language of words and pictures that hadn't been seen before. The goal of many cartoonists was to be published in *Zap*, but by the time *Zap* #4 came out in 1969, the cast was complete. Spain Rodriguez and Robert Williams were the last invited in, and then there was no more room. "Why take more guys?" asked S. Clay Wilson. "Why split the pie any further? Kind of like an art mafia."

"We had a tremendous amount of artists that just weren't very good that were trying to get in there," said Williams. "Of course Crumb wanted to open it up to everybody. There was an elitist situation to a certain extent, but I don't think it was that much of a deal. We were making good money and there weren't any pages to go around. That was one of the factors."

For their fourth issue, the seven contributors vowed to put freedom of the press to a real test. Wilson's "A Ball in the Bung Hole" took sex and violence to an anatomically absurd conclusion, Spain's "Mara, Mistress of the Void" took lust in space way beyond where Wally Wood left off, but it was Crumb's "Joe Blow" that truly outraged the forces of decency everywhere. His cheery, light-hearted story of incest in suburbia presented such a perverse picture of the nuclear family that the comic was busted almost immediately. Booksellers from Berkeley to New York were arrested for selling and possessing *Zap* #4. The news brought a mixture of triumph and apprehension to *Zap's* creators.

Judge Joel Tyler, of the Criminal Court of the City of New York, issued his opinion on the artistic and moral value of *Zap Comics*. "The cartoon is ugly, cheap and degrading. Its purpose is to stimulate erotic responses, and does not, as claimed, deal with basic realities of life. It is grossly shocking, demeaning the sexual experience by perverting it . . . It is a part of the underworld (sic) press—the growing world of deceit in sex, and it is not reality or honesty, as they often claim it to be. It represents an emotional incapacity to view sex as a basis for establishing genuine human relationships, or as a normal part of the human condition.". . .

When they saw bookstores and distributors getting busted, the Zapsters suspected they might be next. "We just thought we were all going to get arrested somewhere down the line, because there had never been material like this," said Williams. . . .

Wilson took the specter of retaliation as a challenge to go

even further in depicting the naked human psyche. "My idea is not to entertain them but to enlighten them," he said. "Or to make them sick. One or the other. Sometimes it happens simultaneously." Wilson's stories went full bore from the first frame to the last, with new characters and locations thrown into the mix at a hectic pace. "Make it jump! Make it crackle! Blister their irises! F—— their minds up!" said Wilson. "Give them a full plate, you know?" He made efficient use of full-page splash panels, often telling a complicated story in a single frame, which had to be pored over carefully to determine who was doing what to whom. . . .

In the context of those conservative times, they were treading on thin ice, and no one knew for certain if their boldness would boomerang, said Williams. "We knew that we were cutting new territory. You look back at it now; it's just a silly nothing. An underground comic is a silly nothing now, but in 1968, '69, '70, we were really cutting new f——ing territory. We had gone pretty damn far in *Zap*, and we had penetration in our comics, and that was the real forbidden fruit to show sexual penetration. That's what none of the magazines would dare do."

"I always saw the underground comix movement as a sort of extension of the ECs [horror comics of the 1950s]," said Wilson. "In my estimation we were taking it one step further by adding sex and drugs and carnage and stuff. Hence the name underground because they kept them under the counter, or else they were getting busted."

In addition to stomping on sexual taboos, Williams and [comics artist Rick] Griffin and [poster and comics artist Victor] Moscoso wanted to transcend the traditional comic story structure and approach the medium as visual art rather than literature. Crumb and Shelton and Spain were more interested in narrative forms, said Williams. "The very first comics were not insistent on an obvious dialogue. They were more expressing a revolutionary insanity, a psychosis, than they were expressing a literal story structure," he explained. "There was a search for an abstract language in the comics, more than a literal language. So the first couple issues of *Zap*, we were like equal 50-50. Half of us were storytellers, and half of us were graphic artists. The graphic thing is what died out in the mid '70s, and never really regained itself."

Wimmen's Comix

Trina Robbins

Although underground comix of the 1960s gave voice
to some counterculture populations, comic books—
whether mainstream or alternative—failed to contend
seriously with women's issues. Teen romance comics
flourished in these times, but their depiction of
women focused on boy troubles and fashion. Furthermore, many of these superficial tales were the creation of male writers and artists. By the 1970s,
though, feminism and the women's liberation movement redefined the role of women in society. Suddenly, women's issues became a concern of the media,
and hitherto hushed topics such as abortion became
part of a national forum for debate.

In the following article, comic artist Trina Robbins discusses how the liberating atmosphere of the
1970s prompted many female artists and writers to
air their concerns about the successes and limitations
of women's empowerment in America. Through
clever art, satire, and autobiographical narratives,
these women offered an alternative, female-centered
view of society—one far removed from the macho superhero comics and the still decidedly male-focused
"underground comix" scene. According to Robbins,
this new subculture addressed facets of their own experience from the hypocrisy of the counterculture to
lesbianism to being a single parent. Realizing they
were creating something different these authors and
artists went through various names for their collective work, but the most commonly used term is
Wimmen's Comix, a phrase that refutes the common
gender-stereotypes that belong to the word "women"

■

and the acceptance of the nonmainstream connotation of "comix." Wimmen's comix continued to evolve through the 1980s and 1990s and currently enjoy wider distribution and greater recognition than ever before.

BY 1970, THE WOMEN'S LIBERATION MOVEMENT had grown substantial enough to be noticed and reported upon, if not necessarily understood, by the mass media. Headlines from major newspapers read, "Gals Unbutton Their Lib" and "Bra Blitzed!" Sadly, most of the male underground cartoonists understood as little about the new women's movement as the newspapers did, and reacted to what they perceived as a threat by drawing comix filled with graphic violence directed mostly at women. People—especially women people—who criticized this misogyny were not especially welcome in this alternative version of the old boys' club, and were not invited into the comix being produced.

Despite the general male antipathy, 1970 saw an explosion of feminist underground newspapers all over America. They had names like *Tooth and Nail, Everywoman, Ain't I A Woman?, Off Our Backs*, and *Goodbye To All That*. Many lasted only a few issues, though *Off Our Backs* is still being published. The San Francisco Bay Area was a steaming hotbed of feminism, and that year *It Ain't Me, Babe*, the first women's liberation newspaper in America, formed in Berkeley. By the second issue, I had found a place with the paper, drawing covers and comic strips for them.

Aside from its Dylan-esque title, *It Ain't Me, Babe* reflected the anarchistic, counterculture rock-and-roll world of both underground comix and second-wave feminism. No last names were listed on the masthead, and, in fact, there was no official editor or art director. Every three weeks the *It Ain't Me, Babe* collective got together and, often with the aid of controlled substances, laid out the whole paper, hit or miss. This resulted in some pretty odd, but always creative, pages. And because the paper came out every three weeks, even though it only lasted for one intense year, it had more than twenty issues. . . .

Later that year, working with the newspaper collective, I

got together the few women cartoonists I could find and produced the very first all-women comic, also called *It Ain't Me, Babe*, subtitled "Women's Liberation."

Like its namesake paper, the comic was of uneven quality, as were the majority of underground comix then. The diverse contents included a psychedelic comic by Willy Mendes, my strip about the Goddess, a sweetly political two-pager by Lisa Lyons, and caustic comments about enslaved office workers by Michele Brand. In the center was a comic strip, again written collectively, in which Juliet Jones, Daisy Duck, Supergirl, and other characters rebel against their sexist boyfriends. Just as women all over America were doing at the time, they form a consciousness-raising group. Petunia Pig says, "Now I see how I've been kept powerless all these years. Being married to Porky kept me isolated from other women. He was able to define my total reality." And Supergirl adds, "I've always felt I was better than other women because of my super powers and always preferred the company of men. How I was kidding myself! Men have never thought of me as an equal."

Real Female Sexuality

In 1972, two separate groups of California women cartoonists came up with the same idea independently, each unaware of the other's existence. In Laguna Beach, Joyce Farmer and Lyn Chevely (using the pseudonym "Chin Lyvely"), two single-mother artists, reacted against the sexist treatment of women in underground comix by deciding to produce a comic that would deal with real female sexuality. They formed their own publishing company, Nanny Goat Productions, and came up with the outrageous title *Tits 'n' Clits*, featuring the adventures of those "perfectly permeable Peters sisters: Glinda, Wanda, and Fonda," and Mary Multipary, who became, in later issues, Mary Nullipary. The stories were indeed about sex from a woman's point of view—they dealt with such topics as vibrators, menstruation, IUDs, and men who miss the toilet bowl.

Tits 'n' Clits was the second all-women comic book and the first continuing all-women anthology. It lasted a healthy fifteen years, although in 1973, when the owners of the Laguna Beach bookstore that sold it—ironically called Fahrenheit 451—were arrested for selling pornography, Farmer and Chevely changed the name for one issue to *Pandora's Box*. By the time *Pandora's Box* came out in 1973, it carried an ad on its inside back cover for thirteen other feminist underground comix, thereby launching the heyday of women's comics.

One of the best and most horrifying story lines produced by Farmer and Chevely, "The American Dream," ran in *Pandora's Box*. Sensitively drawn by Farmer, it's the feminist's answer to all those love comics that ended with a romantic wedding and a promise of "happily ever after." "The American Dream" is the story of Suzanne, who gave up her promising career as a poet to become the perfect wife, hostess, mother, and gourmet cook. Her not exactly supportive husband ("That was all RIGHT! Next time, though, please add a bit more sage to the game hen stuffing!") doesn't satisfy her sexually or emotionally, and she's too busy meeting the demands of him and her children to write anymore. The story builds in intensity as Suzanne gets more overwhelmed. At the breaking point, she tries reaching out to her husband ("Jonathan, I'd like to have some time alone with you . . . listen to music or something?"), but when he cancels out in favor of his job—*she*, of course, has given up *her* career—leaving her alone with three screaming kids for the weekend, she plans a dramatic and frightening suicide.

Important Issues

The same year that they published *Pandora's Box*, Farmer and Chevely produced one of the most important and underappreciated comic books to come out of the 1970s, *Abortion Eve*. Abortion had just been legalized countrywide. Farmer and Chevely, who were counselors at a women's free clinic, saw the need for a comic that explained abortion clearly and in a way that actually made good reading. With graceful art by Farmer, *Abortion Eve* tells the story of five pregnant Eves who meet at an abortion clinic—Evelyn, the suburban matron; Eva, the flower child; Evie, a troubled teenager; Eve, a feisty, savvy black woman; and Evita, an equally feisty Hispanic woman. They each have a different reason for wanting an abortion: neither Eve nor Evita can afford to add more children to their family, and Evelyn is pregnant with the child of her lover, not her husband, Adam. Poor Eva is simply too much of a space case to be a mother. In the course of the book, their counselor, Mary

Multipary, explains to them, and to the reader, the choices they may have in abortion and in birth control, the legality of abortion, and what to expect during the procedure. . . .

At the same time that Farmer and Chevely were putting together their groundbreaking book, ten women cartoonists gathered in San Francisco to form the Wimmen's Comix Collective. The result of their meeting, *Wimmen's Comix*, arrived at comic-book stores three weeks after *Tits 'n' Clits*. In just two years since the publication of *It Ain't Me, Babe*, there were now enough women cartoonists to put out two different women's underground comix.

Like *Abortion Eve*, the first issue of Wimmen's Comix contained an abortion story, "A Teenage Abortion," by Lora Fountain, along with a sarcastic piece on sexism in the workplace by Lee Marrs and a story about pot and revolution by Sharon Rudahl. If you were part of the counterculture in the early 1970s, pot and revolution were your life. It was a time of communes and collectives, and, not unlike the production process of *It Ain't Me, Babe*, every issue of *Wimmen's Comix* was edited by two women, with much input from a core of contributors. But the results weren't always political. As the years and issues progressed, Lee Marrs drew a satire on every gothic romance ever written, Caryn Leschen produced a page on the toilets of Europe, Dori Seda did stories about her dog, and Melinda Gebbie contributed page after claustrophobic page about her sexual confusion.

Significant Firsts

Wimmen's Comix no. 1 also contained the first autobiographical comic ever published, drawn by Aline Kominsky. Autobiography has since become a staple of comics drawn by women, and big chunks of women's comix tend to be about the artist's dysfunctional family, miserable childhood, fat thighs, and boyfriend problems. Although Kominsky seems to have invented the form, the autobiographical comic actually harkens back to the confessional style of mainstream romance comics. Women do love to share confidences!

My contribution to *Wimmen's Comix* no. 1 was "Sandy Comes Out," the first comic about a lesbian. In Portland, a young art student named Mary Wings read "Sandy Comes

Out," and waxed indignant about what she felt was a hetero-sexual take on lesbianism. Twenty-three years later, she wrote about her reaction for *Gay Comix*:

"The year was 1973. I was a sculpture major in art school. The anti-war movement had led me to feminism, and femi-nism—the concept—led me to lesbianism, the practice. It was a lot less theoretical than it sounds. One day, tired from a night of leafleting and tribadism, thumbing through a *Wimmen's Comix* I came upon Trina Robbins' story 'Sandy Comes Out.' I re-member feeling alienated and angry . . . What about struggle, oppression, and the patriarchy? (Dig it, girls, we still live in a pa-triarchy.) Straight women are oppressing me all over the place—with their male identification and their nipples. Not to mention their boyfriends who—they mention—want to watch."

Wings decided, "I'll write *Come Out Comix* and tell it like it is." *Come Out Comix*, self-published by Wings on an offset press, was the first lesbian comic book ever produced. . . .

In Southern California, Roberta Gregory also noticed the rampant heterosexuality of the first *Wimmen's Comix*, and re-acted by drawing "A Modern Romance," which appeared in *Wimmen's* two years later. By 1976, Gregory had self-published her own solo comic, *Dynamite Damsels*, the first of a long, varied line of comic books she continues to produce.

Being published in *Wimmen's Comix* encouraged women cartoonists to go on and produce their own comic books. Some who did so were Sharon Rudahl, Aline Kominsky, Melinda Gebbie, and Dori Seda. Being published in *It Ain't Me, Babe* had given me the courage I needed, and before the first *Wimmen's Comix* hit the stands, I had already put together *All Girl Thrills*, along with Willy Mendes and one Jewelie Goodvibes (remember, this was 1971!), and my own *Girl Fight* comics, while Mendes had produced the psychedelic *Illuminations*.

New Images, New Directions

Feminists at that time were not exactly crazy about the use of the word *girl* in my titles. The new thinking was that *girl* was a demeaning term, just as boy had been a demeaning term for black men. I was attempting irony in my use of that word, but I didn't realize that I was about twenty years too early. In fact, *Wimmen's Comix* was criticized for keeping the word *men* in its title. Feminists were experimenting with new ways to spell their gender, such as *womon* or *womyn*.

A year after the first *Wimmen's Comix*, Lee Marrs came out with *Pudge, Girl Blimp*, a series that lasted through the decade. Pudge was a chronicle of the 1970s in Berkeley, and Marrs's busy, *Mad Comics*-inspired style turned it into a tossed salad of women's groups, communes, Patty Hearst, sex, drugs, and rock and roll. Into this mixture came Pudge, fat as her name implies, seventeen years old, and still a virgin. The little runaway from Normal, Illinois, dressed in a fringed jacket and frayed bellbottoms, is a far cry from [tame 1940s comic maiden] Patsy Walker. "Gee whiz!" she exclaims, wandering blissfully through a crowd of rioting demonstrators, Hare Krishnas, and serial killers, "San Francisco! Enlightenment! Dope! Getting laid! Far out!" Everyone who had come to San Francisco since the Summer of Love, with flowers in their hair, could righteously dig it.

It Ain't Me, Babe, Wimmen's Comix, and the first issue of *Pudge, Girl Blimp* were all published by Last Gasp, a major San Francisco publisher of underground comix. In 1976, Denis Kitchen, a longtime underground cartoonist himself, and president of Kitchen Sink, a midwestern underground comix company, saw how well women's comics were selling, and asked me to put together a women's anthology comic for his company. I didn't want to resurrect *It Ain't Me, Babe*, and *Wimmen's* already existed as a feminist anthology, but, I realized, male cartoonists had been dealing with their often warped views of sex in their comics for a decade. Perhaps it was time for women to explore our own eroticism on the comics page. The result was *Wet Satin*, subtitled "Women's Erotic Fantasies."

Wet Satin provided an exhilarating experience for the women who worked on it, giggling as they drew. For a book with a single theme (sex), the stories were amazingly varied, from Lee Marrs's outdoorsy fantasies with sexy anthropomorphic birds and animals to Melinda Gebbie's nightmare of a beautiful epileptic in Charendon, a madhouse, during the French Revolution. . . .

The book almost immediately ran into trouble. Kitchen's midwestern printer took one look at the book, declared it pornographic, and flatly refused to touch it. This was interesting, considering that the same printer had printed an all-male sex book published by Kitchen featuring such an obscene cover it had to be covered with plain white paper before it could even be distributed to the comic stores. The printer insisted that the male sex book, *Bizarre Sex*, was satire, while *Wet Satin* was serious and therefore objectionable. . . .

Wet Satin finally got printed in the sexually liberal San Francisco, but when we had to go through the same problem with the second issue, putting out a comic about women's sexuality became too much of an uphill battle, and the second issue was its last.

A result of the 1960s sexual liberation was the unstable 1970s family structure. People lived communally, monogamy was often considered "bourgeois," and few marriages lasted. I was a single parent, as were most of the mothers I knew. In 1978, inspired by the way *Abortion Eve* had managed to entertain while educating, I put together *Mama! Dramas*, with eight other women cartoonists who were also mothers, most of them single mothers. Our goal was to show the kind of motherhood that didn't exist in *The Ladies Home Journal.* We drew stories about communal living, alternative schools, playgroups, single parenting, and the realities of being on welfare.

Delores Thom's 1978 story "LEISURELY Welfare Living" demonstrates to the 1990s reader that "welfare reform" is not a new concept. Mary is hardly the welfare queen made famous in Republican mythology. Her husband has left her, and she's stuck: "David's got the job, the training, the credit . . . Let's see who wants to hire an ex-housewife!" But the only work she qualifies for, as a checker in a supermarket, won't even cover essentials like child care and medical bills. (Child support as an alternative to dead-end jobs isn't even mentioned in Thom's story. It was just as impossible to collect then as it is now.) Mary applies for welfare. The caseworker gives her a hard time, and her kids recite the anti-welfare myths they've picked up at school: "Sally's mom's on welfare, and some kid at school says she eats out of his dad's pocket!" The grand sum of $356 a month doesn't go far. Her kids beg, "Mama, I wanna take dance lessons," and "Star Wars! Mama please." Her answer: "We can't afford it." Her house is sold, and she and her ex-husband split the equity, which isn't enough to buy another home. She applies for a loan to buy a new house, of course is turned down, and is "economically forced to live in the ghetto." Her caseworker continues to give her a hard time. By the last panel, Mary's check is late, she's out of food, and she stands hunched over the phone, crying, as her caseworker yells at her: "I don't like people like you. You just don't appreciate what you're getting!!"

Anti-Feminist Backlash

Then the 1980s arrived. Ronald Reagan, who did more to popularize the myth of the welfare queen than anyone, was elected president, and the mood of the country changed, almost overnight. In scores of subtle ways, women were urged back into traditional roles of wives and mothers. The media announced that feminism was dead, and that an unmarried woman over thirty had a better chance of getting killed by terrorists than of getting married. The term *politically correct* became a negative buzzword, and the term *postfeminist* was created to describe a new generation of women who, like heroines in the old love comics, found their fulfillment in a home and husband. . . .

By 1985, even the Wimmen's Comix Collective had fallen for the hype and boasted of a "politically incorrect" issue. Editor Diane Noomin, in the 1991 anthology *Twisted Sisters*, proudly identified the original *Twisted Sisters* underground comic book that she and Aline Kominsky had put out in 1976 as "politically incorrect." Symbolic of the antifeminist backlash was *After Shock*, an all-woman underground comix anthology published in 1981. Editor Rebecca Wilson set the tone of the book with her cover, on which a chic woman, more robot than human, sits, sipping coffee on an elegant sofa. Next to her on the table stands her biological clock, which reads one minute to midnight. All around her, atomic explosions and tsunamis destroy the world, while in the background, the baby she never got around to having weeps, "Mommy??" The book stresses that the only way to cure women's dysfunctional lives is for them to have babies. . . .

All was not lost. Gay cartoonist Howard Cruse started *Gay Comix* in 1980. This book, the first gay comic anthology, published and continues to publish many of the best lesbian cartoonists, like Jennifer Camper, Joan Hilty and Cheela Smith.

After four issues, Robert Triptow took over as editor for the remainder of the 1980s, and Andy Mangels has edited it since 1991. When Mangels took over *Gay Comix*, he made the decision to always include an equal number of pages by women and men, and the book continues to be one of the top showcases for both established and new lesbian cartoonists. . . .

Reviving Romance Comics

By the mid-1980s, it had been almost a decade since the publication of the last mainstream comic for girls. Only the unsinkable *Archie* remained for girls to read. Romance comics were long gone but fondly remembered. The classic love comic—style drawing of a woman, tear in her eye, agonizing over *something*—a lost love, a lost job, the baby she forgot to have—appeared on T-shirts, cups, cards, and in advertising . . . everywhere but in comic books. And some women cartoonists missed the girl comics of their youth enough to attempt, with varying degrees of success, to revive them.

In 1985, Barb Rausch and *Katy Keene*–creator Bill Woggon produced *Vicki Valentine* for independent publisher Deni Loubert. It was a contemporary rerun of Woggon's old *Katy Keene* comics, down to the reader-designed clothes and paper dolls. Woggon even made guest appearances in the book, dressed in his familiar cowboy getup, as "Wild Bill Hiccup."

In 1986, I managed to convince Marvel Comics to give teen comics another try with my six-part series *Meet Misty*, and when that ended I produced *California Girls*, an eight-part teen series, for the independent publisher Eclipse. At the same time, Barbara Slate had talked DC Comics into publishing her girl comic *Angel Love*. Although all these books received enthusiastic mail from comic-hungry girls across the country, none lasted over a year. Loubert and I even made a brief attempt to bring back a more contemporary version of love comics in 1987, when I edited two issues of *Renegade Romance* for her company, Renegade Press. But it had been too long since women and girls had bought comics. Comic shops, the only places to buy comics in the 1980s, were filled with superhero comics, and had become the sole province of boys.

Evolving Black Identity in Superhero Comics

Marc Singer

In the following selection, Marc Singer examines the portrayal of black characters in superhero comics. Before drawing his own conclusions, Singer reviews the existing literature on race and comics, much of which argues that comics have traditionally reinforced common stereotypes about race and ethnicity and therefore trap black superheroes between autonomy and the restrictions imposed by social conventions. While acknowledging that the tension exists, Singer believes that many contemporary comics authors choose to reflect this struggle in their black superheroes. The result is a cast of complex characters whose normal lives and superhero personas represent the split identity that defines the minority experience in America. Using examples of modern black superheroes, Singer illustrates how this novel character construction brings to light "the dilemmas of racial and other minority groups" for the possibly unenlightened readership. It also challenges the use of black superheroes to add token diversity to a mainly white, male super-club—a tactic that was prevalent in the 1970s and 1980s and is still all too common today. Marc Singer is an assistant professor of English at Tennessee State University.

■

Marc Singer, "'Black Skins' and White Masks: Comic Books and the Secret of Race," *African American Review*, vol. 36, Spring 2002, p. 107. Copyright © 2002 by Marc Singer. Reproduced by permission.

THE STEREOTYPES THROUGH WHICH AMERICAN popular culture often interprets and represents racial identity operate not only as tools of defamation but also as vehicles for far more subtle manipulations of race. In his 1946 essay "Twentieth-Century Fiction and the Black Mask of Humanity," Ralph Ellison observes that stereotypes of African Americans, whatever other purposes they might serve, become a means "by which the white American seeks to resolve the dilemma arising . . . between his acceptance of the sacred democratic belief that all men are created equal and his treatment of every tenth man as though he were not"—a means, in other words, of reconciling the contradictions between an ideology of democracy and a history and practice of prejudice. Whether these stereotypes assume the form of unrealistic portrayals of racial minorities or an equally unrealistic invisibility, they often fulfill this double function of oppression and reaffirmation.

Comic books, and particularly the dominant genre of superhero comic books, have proven fertile ground for stereotyped depictions of race. Comics rely upon visually codified representations in which characters are continually reduced to their appearances, and this reductionism is especially prevalent in superhero comics, whose characters are wholly externalized into their heroic costumes and aliases. This system of visual typology combines with the superhero genre's long history of excluding, trivializing, or "tokenizing" minorities to create numerus minority superheroes who are marked purely for their race: "Black Lightning," "Black Panther," and so forth. The potential for superficiality and stereotyping here is dangerously high. Yet in recent years, some comics creators have demonstrated that the superhero genre's own conventions can invite a more nuanced depiction of minority identity. Race in contemporary comics proves to be anything but simplistic. If some titles reveal deceptively soothing stereotypes lurking behind their veneers of diversity, then others show complex considerations of identity. . . .

Where Do Stereotypes Reside?

Historically, critics have long associated comics with the perpetuation of racial stereotypes. Frantz Fanon forges this connection in passing in *Black Skins, White Masks* (1967), writing,

"Look at the children's picture magazines: Out of every Negro mouth comes the ritual 'Yassuh, boss'". Fredric Wertham had offered far more extensive criticisms in *Seduction of the Innocent* (1954), in which he argues that comics "expose children's minds to an endless stream of prejudice-producing images" in which whites are always handsome and heroic whereas non-whites are inferior and subhuman. Wertham believes these representations not only motivate individual readers toward prejudice, but affect society as a whole by normalizing racist standards through repetition. This process of normalization and indoctrination is, Wertham writes, "where a psychiatric question becomes a social one". Yet the writings of Wertham, Fanon, and other early critics of comics stereotypes tend to apply this formulation only in reverse: Beginning with the social problems of racism in society, they arrive at a condemnation of the internal oppressions comics construct within readers' minds.

Fanon proclaims that "to make [a black man] talk pidgin is to fasten him to the effigy of him, to snare him, to imprison him, the eternal victim of an essence, of an appearance for which he is not responsible", casting the imprisonment as a psychological, existential sentence rather than a social one. Even Wertham, who concludes that the negative images in comics stem from "not an individual condition of children, but a social condition of adults", nevertheless centers his arguments on the psychological harm comics wreak on individual readers. . . .

This sort of psychological criticism has come under sharp attack by Martin Barker in *Comics: Ideology, Power, and the Critics* (1989). Barker argues that criticisms of stereotypes in comics, especially those which imply that stereotypes exert some manner of influence over readers, are built upon a shallow understanding of comics. For Barker, these criticisms rest upon "an unsupportable distinction between textual messages and devices"; in other words, they consider racial images purely as ideological messages transmitted by the comics, whereas Barker considers these same images as generic types which draw upon comic-book conventions rather than racial beliefs. Barker claims that comics incorporate racial stereotypes so fully into their conventions that the images become mere formal devices:

Just because a witch-doctor appears, it does not mean he can be directly related to the mythical witch-doctor of racist legend; he is a witch-doctor within the transforming laws and structure of [the comics]. Therefore he can "reinforce" nothing.

Barker rightly challenges any criticism which presumes that comics hold a deceptive, seductive power over a completely passive audience. In doing so, however, he also drastically isolates comics from their own content, never considering that comics might retain meanings or connotations beyond their own generic and formal functions. . . .

One Contradiction Among Many

The issue of race in comics needs a less dogmatic approach, one which can set aside claims that stereotypes govern readers' minds while still holding comics accountable for their ideological assumptions. Ian Gordon offers such an approach in *Comic Strips and Consumer Culture, 1890–1945* (1998), one chapter of which traces the appearance, and the disappearance, of African American stereotypes in American humor magazines and comic strips. Gordon argues that the same racist humor which stereotyped African Americans in minstrelsy also prevented those stereotypes from fueling successful comic strips; for Gordon, financially successful strips had to be "poly-semic", capable of being read with a multiplicity of meanings, a trait which the reductive stereotypes of racialist discourse lacked. Comic-strip creators were forced to deracinate black stereotypes in order to give their humor more widespread appeal; Gordon suggests that "funny animal figures" like Felix the Cat, Krazy Kat, and, perhaps, Mickey Mouse, possess characteristics of trickery, innocence, and dumb luck which "owed something to stereotypes of African Americans".

Other critics have delivered similar readings. In *Comics as Culture* (1990), M. Thomas Inge writes that

Comic book heroes also tend to fit most of the classic patterns of heroism in Western culture. . . . Spider-Man belongs to the trickster tradition among folk heroes. . . . It is interesting to note that the trickster figure in African folklore is often a spider. Most of the heroes of the world of comic books likewise fit these patterns which are as old as Western civilization.

Yet African folklore is not Western civilization, as "the West" is traditionally defined; Spider-Man, like the funny-animal tricksters before him, may incorporate an African and African American character type, transmuting it into a deracinated comic-book image. Inge is nevertheless accurate when he asserts that "comic books have continued to maintain and develop these patterns [of cultural lore], translate them into forms more suitable to a post-industrial society"; racial images may be yet another "pattern" incorporated into the fabric of comics, through the processes Inge and Gordon describe.

In his book *Super Heroes: A Modern Mythology* (1992), Richard Reynolds offers an acute, if brief, analysis of the role race plays in superhero comics. Reynolds finds it difficult to ascribe one particular ideological function to minority characters because he views the superhero as a multivalent sign which "supports a varied and contradictory battery of readings. He is both the exotic and the agent of order which brings the exotic to [the comic] book". Such contradictions always lie at the heart of superhero comics for Reynolds, who takes an almost textbook structuralist approach in defining the genre as the product of numerous internal conflicts and tensions. These tensions result in a sort of equilibrated stasis which, according to Reynolds, "has made it difficult for black superheroes to inscribe any ideological values of their own"; instead they are absorbed into the generic ideology of the superhero, in which exotic outsiders—and few are so exotic in the comics as black superheroes—work to preserve America's status quo. Any examination of race in superhero comics must consider these innate tensions, as the handling of race is forever caught between the genre's most radical impulses and its most conservative ones.

Skin-Deep Diversity

One such contradiction can be seen in the long-running DC Comics series *Legion of Super-Heroes*. Created in 1958, the *Legion* has always featured dozens of idealistic super-teens, each hailing from a different planet in the far future; for this reason, *Legion* writers of the 1990s cast the team as a symbol of multicultural cooperation and diversity. Yet upon closer examination, this diversity proves to be only skin-deep.

For nearly twenty years, the Legion's supposed racial diversity was mitigated—if not virtually negated—by the fact that, of all the races represented in the comic, only one group existed in real life: the white characters who comprised the bulk of the Legion. The first nonwhite characters were Brainiac 5, who was colored green only because of his connection to the preexisting Superman villain Brainiac, and Chameleon Boy, a shape-shifting alien with the ability to assume any appearance at will. Chameleon Boy would become the start of a long *Legion* tradition of locating racial difference in characters of no fixed physical form. In general, however, the Legion represented race in a manner very typical of Silver Age comics, replacing Earthly races with alien ones who differed from the normative white characters only in the exotic pastel colors of their skin.

In the April 1976 story "The Hero Who Hated the Legion" (*Superboy* no. 216), for example, four members of the Legion of Super-Heroes meet an African superhero named Tyroc and induce him to join their organization with this appeal: "When it comes to race, we're colorblind! Blue skin, yellow skin, green skin . . . we're brothers and sisters . . . united in the name of justice everywhere!" The Legionnaires cite their own skin colors as proof of their inclusivity. Significantly, no race is assigned to the first character in the tableau, the white Superboy; even though he hails from an alien planet, his white skin normalizes him and, by the logic of the comic, marks him as not belonging to any "race." The character Karate Kid, who was represented as Asian during artist Mike Grell's tenure, is presumably the bearer of the "yellow skin"— such was the cultural sensitivity of 1970s comic books—while the other two characters are racialized by their blue and green skins. Both "races" are patently fictitious, yet it is their inclusion which permits the *Legion's* easy but hollow claim to racial harmony. This practice of locating racial difference only among fictional, alien races was assailed by Denny O'Neil in an historic issue of *Green Lantern/Green Arrow* (no. 76 [Apr. 1970]), in which an elderly black man righteously tells Green Lantern:

I been readin' about you . . . how you work for the blue skins
. . . and how on a planet someplace you helped out the orange
skins . . . and you done considerable for the purple skins! Only
there's skins you never bothered with—! . . . The black skins!

In other words, superhero comics represented every fantastic race possible, as a means of ignoring real ones.

With the introduction of Tyroc, however, the Legion
gradually expanded to include members of more extant, nonwhite races and cultures: Writers introduced a Native American Legionnaire, and retroactively determined another member was Jewish. Mike Grell was already drawing the Karate
Kid with Asian features, although subsequent artists would return to his original, Caucasian appearance. If the 1970s' vogue
for socially relevant comic books encouraged just this sort of
artificial tokenism, it nevertheless gave the Legion's diversity
some real-world referents; and if the Legion's roots were still
racially homogenous, then everybody pretended not to notice.

In the 1990s, however, two *Legion* writers decided they
wouldn't settle for diversifying the Legion's future—they
wanted to integrate its past. Tom and Mary Bierbaum retroactively wrote a black character named Kid Quantum into the
Legion's early history (*Legion* no. 33 [Sep. 1992]). But Kid
Quantum was not all that he seemed; the young black man was
actually a Protean, yet another species of shape-shifting alien.
This undercut the Bierbaums' goal of diversification, and
added yet another fantastic race to the Legion's ranks. The *Legion* writers had once again decided, as had earlier writers with
Chameleon Boy, that their emblem of racial difference would
be a character who could pass as any race.

Interestingly, both Kid Quantum and Chameleon Boy belong to races which suffer from discrimination even in the en-
lightened future of *Legion of Super-Heroes*. Chameleon Boy is a
Durlan, one of a race that is all but quarantined to its home
world because other planets fear the Durlans' shape-shifting
abilities; in a 1994 issue, even one of the Legionnaires says,
"Durlans aren't allowed to roam free on Earth! Lousy morphs
can't be trusted!" The Proteans had an even worse lot: For
decades, other races viewed them as unintelligent house pets,
only recently acknowledging their sentience. These histories of

discrimination are signs that *Legion* writers have tried to address real-world issues of racial difference through allegories of science fiction: It is the discrimination, sadly enough, that fleshes out the Durlans and Proteans as distinctly different races. Unlike most of the Legion's "alien" species, which tend to be depicted as white Americans from the 1950s, these shape-shifters bear a racial overdetermination enforced upon them by other species. However, these shape-shifters also demonstrate that, for nearly forty years, *Legion* writers equated any racial difference with complete racial indeterminacy and mutability. The same characters who most clearly exhibit racial difference in the Legion's future are also given the powers to collapse all racial boundaries, and the "difference" with which they are branded in their world becomes virtually meaningless in ours. . . .

In his 1993 novel *Japanese by Spring*, Ishmael Reed characterizes race relations in America with a metaphor that, significantly, draws its vehicle from the comics:

> It was usually the whites and the blacks who were seeking separation from each other, though any examination of American culture would show that they couldn't do without each other and that the blacks had become a sort of Schmoo of American culture, Al Capp's creature, who was an all-purpose thing. You could hate it, love it, exploit it, despise it, enjoy it.

Legion of Super-Heroes enacts this metaphor in a surrealistically literal manner; the Bierbaums and other writers create diversity in the Legion's future by locating it in protean characters who serve as free-floating signifiers for the racial "other" without representing any real-world races. In this sense, *Legion of Super-Heroes* perfectly illustrates the contradictory treatment of race in many superhero comics: Torn between sci-fi fantasy and cultural reality, *Legion* ultimately erases all racial and sexual differences with the very same characters that it claims analogize our world's diversity.

Split Identities and Double Lives

Some writers, however, have used superhero comics to address race and identity with greater, rather than lesser, complexity. Tony Isabella's short-lived 1995 run of *Black Lightning* provides one such example. Black Lightning always was one of the more postmodern black superheroes; even the afro he sported in the 1970s was merely a wig worn to conceal his secret identity. And this concept of the secret identity lies at the heart of how some recent comics have capitalized on, rather than been confined by the contradictions of, the superhero genre's conventions in representing issues of race.

Richard Reynolds includes the secret identity as one of his seven definitive traits of superheroes, but burying it in a list may not adequately convey the important role that the secret identity plays in distinguishing superheroes from other genres of popular culture. The secret identity, and particularly its public component, the costumed identity, is the most readily apparent trait that unites such disparate characters as the alien Superman, the god Thor, and the strictly human Batman in the category of "superhero." Even characters whose identities are publicly known, like the Hulk or the Fantastic Four, often have a noticeable and visually characterized division between their private selves and their public, costumed identities; indeed, the Hulk alternates between two entirely different bodies. Thus, superhero identities need not be secret, but they should be split, to maintain the contrast of "the extraordinary nature of the hero . . . with the mundane nature of his alter-ego".

The idea of the split identity, one of the most definitive and distinctive traits of the superhero, is also one of the most powerful and omnipresent figures used to illustrate the dilemmas and experiences of minority identity. The concept has a long pedigree in theories of race, beginning in 1903 with W.E.B. Du Bois's *The Souls of Black Folk* and his concepts of the veil and double-consciousness. In describing the psychological tolls of institutionalized racism, Du Bois writes,

> The Negro is a sort of seventh son, born with a veil, and gifted with second-sight in this American world,—a world which yields him no true self-consciousness, but only lets him see himself through the revelation of the other world. It is a peculiar sensation, this double-consciousness, this sense of always looking at one's self through the eyes of others. . . . One ever feels his two-ness,—an American, a Negro; two souls, two thoughts, two unreconciled strivings; two warring ideals in one dark body.

Fanon casts this divided self in more existential terms in *Black Skin, White Masks;* in the chapter on "The Fact of Blackness," he describes how white onlookers continually reinscribe their concept of black identity upon him through their racist observations—all of which boil down to a little girl's cry of "'Look, a Negro!'" As a result of this overdetermination from without, Fanon argues, "the Negro has been given two frames of reference within which he has had to place himself", and the black psyche becomes split.

Nor is this psychological split unique to racial groups. In his book *Disidentifications* (1999), José Esteban Muñoz offers a theory of identity which is not limited to race, but also considers other distinctions such as sexuality and gender. Attempting to both refute and balance essentialist and social-constructivist narratives of identity formation, Muñoz regards identity as "a site of struggle where fixed dispositions clash against socially constituted definitions", a conflict and interaction between the internal and external visions of the self. In a sense, Muñoz offers a more poststructurally savvy but equally dialectical version of Du Bois's account of minority identity formation; Fanon, too, refuses to relegate race to either an "essence" or a social construction and attempts to balance both in his existential phenomenology. All three writers structure identity as a conflict between or emergence from the individual and social conceptions of the self. This dual or dialectical origin leads easily to divided identities, especially when the conflict between the individual and social constructions is extreme—as it is when racial, sexual, and other minorities encounter prejudiced, hateful, ignorant, or overdetermining social constitutions of their identity.

Significantly, Muñoz regards comic books as a major site for representing, transforming, and "disidentifying" cultural images of racial and sexual identity. He suggests, for example, that Superman is a racial mediation between anti-Semitic myths of the Ubermensch and Jewish cultural tropes. I would further argue that the superhero genre itself supports such racial negotiations through its central convention of the split identity—a convention which perfectly mimics the dialectical, existential, or differential split which Du Bois, Fanon, and Muñoz ascribe to racial and other categories of minority identity. The secret identity provides a perfect narrative means for exploring these real-life split identities. As an aside, the identities of the Legion of Super-Heroes are among the least split in comics; the characters have civilian names but otherwise tend to show little difference between their superhero and civilian selves. Perhaps the *Legion* comics' bizarre erasure of race has emerged, in part, because they effectively lack the concept which has been fundamental to the representation of minority identity, both in comic books and in critical race theory.

Tony Isabella, however, shows a keen awareness of costumes and split identities in *Black Lightning* no.5 (June 1995). In this issue, Black Lightning has just been attacked in his secret identity as schoolteacher Jefferson Pierce; Walter Kasko, a fellow teacher, has died saving a young student while Pierce stood by paralyzed. As Pierce languishes in the hospital, he cannot tell the doctors that his depression stems from his failure to act as a superhero when the situation demanded it—a conventional enough split-identity dilemma.

However, Pierce learns that Walter Kasko had secrets of his own when he meets Samuel Daly, a hospital lab worker who was Walter's lover. Samuel draws a connection between their homosexuality and Pierce's double life, telling Pierce, "Some of us keep our secrets better than others. But you know all about secrets, don't you?" Isabella then further analogizes superheroics to homosexuality when Samuel tells Pierce that a doctor "ordered a metagene test. . . . The records will show you tested negative. I figure Walter would have wanted it that way". This conjures ominous shades of an HIV test; while a "positive" result on the metagene test would not reveal a life-threatening virus, it would effectively end the "Jefferson Pierce" life by destroying its separation from Pierce's costumed career as Black Lightning. Thus, in the pages of *Black Lightning*, where we might expect to see a treatment of superheroes and race, Isabella has also associated superheroism and homosexuality. Both, Isabella says, can lead to secret identities and double lives—an analogy entirely consistent with Muñoz's analysis of the dialectical divisions within both queer and nonwhite identity. . . .

Because superhero comics have evolved their own conventions for representing the dilemmas of a divided self, they have the potential to become perfect vehicles for exploring minority-group identity; similarly, from the perspective of the comics, minority groups may be ideal subjects for these same reasons. Superhero comics can literally personify the otherwise abstract ontological divides of minority identity, assigning each self its own visual identifier, its own body, and then charting the effects as these bodies house and are housed by the same mind. Those few comics writers who already use the superhero split identity to portray this aspect of minority identity generally present race and sexuality with richness and complexity, free of the tokenism and erasure which have dominated the genre.

Trapped Between Constructed Identities

Tony Isabella is one such writer, another is Christopher Priest, who with artist Chris Cross infused the short-lived series *Xero* (1997–98) with a constant awareness of race and identity. Xero is Coltrane Walker, a black government agent forced by his superiors to disguise himself as a blondhaired, blue-eyed superhero. In his other cover identity, Walker is a rough–and-tumble basketball player; a mock sports-magazine article written for *Xero* no. 8 says Walker's fans are "a range of loks [street gang members], OG's [gang toughs], murderous felons" and calls Walker himself "a thug. A deviant. Six feet, six inches, 220 pounds of militant black rage that no legitimate NBA team would touch". Walker is thus trapped between two highly artificial and mutually exclusive roles, the black gangsta basketball player and the Aryan superspy, and the series chronicles his attempts to rebuild some sort of inner life between the demands of these two stereotypes. Priest and Cross constantly exploit this racial duality; one of Cross's most recurrent images depicts Xero with half of his white face ripped off, revealing the black face underneath. Cross frequently leaves the top of Xero's mask and his cybernetic eye intact, allowing the superhero costume and the nonhuman, cyborg identity to mediate or provide a transition between the black and white faces.

Priest is no less aware of this racial division and its connection to superhero convention. In issue no. 6, Xero defeats the supervillain Dr. Polaris—who himself suffers from a split personality which pits his civilian and costumed selves against one another—by removing his costume and white skin, revealing his true appearance. Xero tells Polaris, "I'm a man of two distinct personas—just like you", a comparison which suggests that Xero's own identities may be just as antagonistic as Polaris's. In this same issue, Xero is attacked by fearful villagers who mistake his costumed persona for a supervillain; by issue's end they are only too eager to assist the internationally famous basketball star Coltrane Walker. *Xero* no. 6 implies that Walker's undisguised black identity is healthier and perhaps even more heroic than his white, superhero one and the internal conflicts it creates. Such a story is typical of the middle of *Xero*'s run, in which Priest begins hinting that the costume and its false identity ultimately do Walker more harm than good.

The next two issues are flashbacks which chronicle Xero's origin and the creation of his false identity. When Xero's agency rebuilds his body after a catastrophic injury, their final addition is his white mask. A rival agent named One delivers the mask and mockingly tells Xero, "Think of it as kind of backwards affirmative action, Bro". One's irony does not obscure Priest's point: The agency is attempting to program Xero's loyalty by subsuming him into an artificial racial identity and then testing his devotion to it. Their final test, a test which Xero repeatedly fails, requires him to repeat on command the racial slur "Niggers sho' is stupid". Were he ever to pass the test, it would mark his complete abandonment of any internal racial identity which is not controlled by the agency. This test also suggests that both of the identities the agency supplies, the white mask and the black "thug," are based on overdetermined, racist stereotypes of African Americans; Walker's assumption of the white Xero identity is contingent on his recitation of the slur. Thus, the fabricated identities in Xero are not simply social constructions, they are also instruments of societal control.

Priest escalates this idea of identity fabrication throughout the series. In the grand finale, he reveals that no one is what he or she seems: One, who has been posing as an Asian man for years, turns out to be a woman of indeterminate race, and Draza, the comic's major villain, turns out to be a facade for Frank Decker, Xero's boss. Gender, political allegiance, and morality prove as easily manipulable as race, and the only lesson, if we can extract one, seems to be that these manipulations usually serve the ends of mysterious authority figures like Decker. *Xero* posits that all categories of identity, including race, can in fact be mutable constructions built upon externally imposed stereotypes. In this sense, the series presents a nightmarish version of Muñoz's schema, in which all identities are assigned by external, social pressures. Whereas Tony Isabella saw the split identity as an opportunity to analogize and praise superheroes and minority groups, Priest views the concealed identity as a deadly charade with devastating moral consequences. Both writers, however, portray the psychological costs of split identities, using superhero conventions to represent metaphorically the dilemmas of racial and other minority groups. . . .

Many of Wertham's allegations remain relevant today: Comics still perpetuate stereotypes, either through token characters who exist purely to signify racial cliches or through a far more subtle system of absence and erasure that serves to obscure minority groups even as the writers pay lip service to diversity. However, superhero comics also possess a highly adaptable set of conventions; a few titles display the genre's and the medium's potential by using the generic vocabulary of the secret identity to externalize and dramatize the conditions of minority identity in America. In so doing, these comics also demonstrate that the concepts of double-consciousness and divided identity remain artistically viable techniques for representing race, as valid in the popular culture of today as they were in Du Bois's study nearly one hundred years ago.

EXAMINING POP CULTURE

New Forms for a Contemporary Audience

Serious Comics and Graphic Novels: True Art for Adults

David Thompson

In late 1986, two comic book miniseries appeared that would revolutionize the content of a medium that was primarily aimed at teen audiences. Frank Miller's *The Dark Knight Returns* and Alan Moore and Dave Gibbons's *Watchmen* presented dark images of superhero worlds in which the psychological, moral, and political dimensions of crime fighting came to the fore. Aided by jarring artwork, these titles undermined the superhero mythology by creating characters that were no longer champions of justice, but rather obsessed avengers and damaged demigods confused by their own omnipotence. Working outside the black-and-white ethics of most superhero comics allowed these inventive writers and artists to create fictional societies that mirrored the real world and thus opened up a new channel for social satire and human drama.

In the following article, David Thompson discusses the new direction comic books took with the advent of these two influential series. According to Thompson, by taking on mature subject matter and more dystopian themes, these darker comics reached the level of serious art—offering more social criticism and personal reflection than other contemporary

■

forms of supposed high art. Both *The Dark Knight Returns* and *Watchmen* were collected into single volumes, helping to jumpstart a new industry trend toward producing trade paperbacks (TPBs) and graphic novels. Trade paperbacks are book-format collections of comic books originally printed as separate issues of a series. Graphic novels are unique, self-contained stories presented in a comic-book format. Printed and bound like high-quality books, TPBs and graphic novels can just as easily be found in large bookstores as tiny comics shops. Consequently, they reached a larger audience, and the readership age of comics went up as more adults reembraced a love that was commonly sacrificed at the end of childhood. David Thompson is the cofounder of Emit Records, a music label. He also works as a freelance writer who covers music, film, and other pop-culture topics.

SIX MONTHS AFTER [FILMMAKER] BRYAN SINGER'S *X-Men* translated its comic-book source as science fiction rather than cartoonish camp, superhuman heroism is also the central intrigue of [filmmaker] M. Night Shyamalan's newly released postmodern puzzler, *Unbreakable.* That both films find unexpected resonance in such subject matter reflects a recent—and equally curious—reinvention of the comic book itself. In the early 1980s, the future of the comic-book superhero seemed grim. The expansive optimism of the 1950s, with monthly sales in excess of 100 million copies, had been replaced by creative ennui and commercial desperation. Although still faster than a speeding bullet, decades of crime-fighting had left the costumed adventurer dull and blunted, out of step with smaller, more cynical times. Mainstream comic books seemed kitsch and ridiculous, their heroes rendered impotent not by kryptonite or ray guns, but by irrelevance and laughter.

Industry Transformation

Faced with an indifferent audience and falling sales, the comic-book industry was forced to abandon its scattergun approach of innumerable throwaway titles aimed at mainstream newsagents and the casual reader. Instead, the major publishers began dealing directly with an emerging network of smaller and more knowledgeable specialist retailers who, in turn, dealt primarily with adult collectors and fellow comic-book obsessives. This streamlined system proved far more efficient, with print runs informed by rapid and more detailed feedback. Marginal titles with low print runs began to pay for themselves, no longer requiring subsidy from the sale of merchandising and major titles, consequently, publishers could entertain riskier, more ambitious projects, shifting attention to an older and more discriminating readership, referred to by the industry as "intense customers". In 1986, the comic book began a transformation worthy of its own pages, as two such risky projects redefined what the medium could be. Significantly, both titles proceed from the same basic premise: what if superheroes lived in a world like ours, an untidy world, where actions have consequences and heroic ideals seem incongruous, quixotic or absurd? What would that reveal about them? What would it reveal about us?

The Dark Knight Returns

In an attempt to restore meaning and mythical resonance to one of DC's oldest and most famous characters, Frank Miller's four-part mini-series, *The Dark Knight Returns*, vividly captured the zeitgeist in that decade. An ageing, isolated Batman emerges from retirement to curb the escalating violence of Gotham city's urban gangs and, in so doing, is forced to take increasingly desperate measures. Fragments of media commentary punctuate the unfolding events, its figures continuing to debate Batman's methods and motives while, around them, civilisation crumbles. Stark, visceral and often surreal, Miller's illustrations evoke a sense of grotesque disorder, from a monstrously armoured Batmobile to the Joker's exploding airborne baby dolls. Yet many of the most potent moments in the series depict smaller acts of violence and the practised impotence of passers-by. The inhabitants of Miller's Gotham are ultimately threatened not by outlandish super-villains, but by a shrivelling of their own moral senses—a dark night of the soul—as indifference and brutality become tools of everyday survival.

With its parallel depictions of adolescent nihilism and adult bad faith—one reflecting the other—*The Dark Knight Returns* remains an uncomfortable reminder of our own disconnection from inspirational ideals.

The Price of Action

The opening pages of Alan Moore's *Watchmen* suggest that its heroes, too, are out of place, the faded artefacts of a bygone age. Most have retired, but one has been murdered, and a dishevelled vigilante called Rorschach suspects he and his erstwhile colleagues are in danger of calculated extinction. Essentially a detective story told from multiple points of view, its 12-issue format marks a countdown to Armageddon, as the world teeters on the brink of thermonuclear war. The looming insanity of the superpowers could be prevented by a character with superpowers of his own, the casually miraculous Dr. Manhattan. Freakishly disembodied by a laboratory mishap, Dr. Manhattan is, literally, a self-resurrected man. All but omnipotent, this blue, transfigured being is assumed to be America's deliverance, a quantum mechanical marvel and the ultimate deterrent. However, the doctor's numinous perceptions are proving incompatible with human imperatives: "A live body and a dead body contain the same number of particles. Structurally, there's no discernible difference. Life and death are unquantifiable abstracts. Why should I be concerned?"

To attempt to summarise *Watchmen*'s labyrinthine plot adequately would be to miss its point entirely, because much of the comic's poetry lies in the counterpoint and convergence of its parallel narratives and visual motifs. In keeping with its themes of surveillance, symmetry and time, the story emerges from a multiplicity of perspectives, incorporating flashbacks, found correspondence and precognitive clues. (Chapter nine takes place on the red planet Mars, while the governments of its blue neighbour stand poised at DEFCON 2. As Dr. Manhattan explains his metaphysical indifference to the distant human drama, an incidental remark offers a striking, if partial, glimpse of what will follow: "I return to the Earth at some point in my future. The streets are full of corpses. The details are vague . . . Beyond that, events grow sketchier: I am standing in deep snow . . . I am killing someone. Their identity is uncertain. . . .") Unprecedented in its structural complexity and density of reference, *Watchmen* dwarfed all expectations of the medium, attracting high praise from *Newsweek, Time* and *Rolling Stone*, publications not previously known for their critical interest in comic books. As subsequent readings reveal further symmetries and detail, it is not entirely surprising that several academic websites are devoted to exhaustive annotation of the 400 pages of the series. Subsequently republished in book form, *Watchmen* is not only a legitimate modern novel, but an insightful and conscientious one, with means, ends, and moral action as its ultimate concerns.

A wave of innovative titles, formats and imprints soon followed, challenging the boundaries of comic-book form and content. Curiously, the talent reinventing this archetypal American medium was largely British. Both Moore and his *Watchmen* collaborator Dave Gibbons had previously been involved with the home-grown science-fiction title *2000 AD* and a comic-strip version of the decidedly British *Dr Who*. As publishers noted the artistic and commercial impact of what became known as the "UK invasion", British writers and artists were even invited to tamper with America's most sacred comic-book institutions.

Insanity

Published as a single hardcover volume that sold more than a quarter of a million copies, *Arkham Asylum* became one of the more surprising commercial successes of 1989. Written by Grant Morrison, with remarkable, macabre paintings by Dave McKean, *Arkham Asylum* transformed Miller's mythical Batman into an almost supernatural figure. Trapped inside Gotham's infamous criminal madhouse, Batman is stalked by an assortment of unhinged and vengeful adversaries while he confronts inner demons of his own. As the lunatics run loose through Arkham's corridors and cellars, theirs is not the only sanity in question. Surrounded by torment and bedlam, the asylum's psychotherapist speaks of seeing positive improvement, her rationalisations little more than amulets to keep the chaos at bay: "We're not even sure if the Joker can be defined as insane. We're beginning to think it may be a neurological disorder, similar to Tourette's Syndrome. It's quite possible we may actually be looking at some kind of brilliant new modification, more suited to urban life at the end of the Twentieth Century . . ." Acknowledging the Gothic mood of Bob Kane's prototypical Batman drawings, Morrison and McKean employ suggestion and psychology, rather than gadgetry and fisticuffs. Defined by the perceptions of those around him, the nocturnal detective is more spectral symbol than man, accordingly rendered in subtle, muted tones and expressionistic shadow, his edges shifting and uncertain. Dark, introspective and visually haunting, *Arkham Asylum* is still the most unearthly interpretation of a hero whose story, on reflection, has always been about ghosts.

Offbeat Perspectives

McKean's illustrative talents were employed to striking effect in Neil Gaiman's oblique and literary Sandman series and *Mr. Punch*, an allegorical tale of puppet-show temptation told with painting, photography and collage, both appearing under DC's Vertigo imprint. Conceived as a showcase for one-off anomalies and more adult-orientated material, Vertigo was set in motion by DC's British talent liaison, Karen Berger. Under Berger's supervision, a number of long-neglected characters were resurrected and given contemporary twists. Vertigo's more successful resuscitations include Grant Morrison's peculiar *Doom Patrol* and an update of Steve Ditko's 1970s curio, *Shade, the Changing Man*. Ditko's strange, erratic tale of interdimensional espionage and mind-warping underwear became, if anything, even odder in its second incarnation, with the writer Peter Milligan describing the story's central themes as "madness and hair". The popularity of such titles confirmed an appetite among readers for offbeat stories, "difficult" subjects and visual innovation.

While Vertigo deconstructed its heroes with varying degrees of postmodern irony, others focused on the emotive and metaphorical possibilities of the costumed adventurer. Combining major scenarios from the 60-year history of Marvel Comics with the almost photorealistic painting of Alex Ross, Kurt Busiek's Nineties graphic novel *Marvels* has as its focus not a string of superhuman dramas, but the human bystanders who witness them. Told entirely from the perspective of a newspaper photographer, the story's enormous span interlinks some of the medium's finest moments. From the Frankenstein undertones of the 1940s Human Torch to the civil rights reflections of *X-Men*, Busiek and Ross address the emotional impact of the fantastic, contrasting panoramic spectacle with notes of awe, fear and alienation. Such is the book's visual opulence and subtlety that the eye lingers over almost every page, absorbing period detail, both real and from its own fictional history. Lovingly crafted and strangely poignant, *Marvels* is no mere chronology of nostalgia, but an existential reminder of a capacity for wonder that adults all too often lose.

The New "Serious" Art

Set against the "serious" contemporary art currently in favour—art that is conspicuously devoid of content or achievement in its construction—these comic books are examples of true modern art. Indeed, *Watchmen*, *Arkham Asylum* and *Marvels* are works of artistic devotion, requiring a lucidity of imagination and a meticulous commitment measured in years—qualities that seem beyond the capabilities of the art world's latest pretenders. Tracey Emin's soiled bed and Sarah Lucas's vaginal kebab jokes are exercises in self-preoccupation, communicating nothing but the nervous vanity of their makers and conforming entirely to an age in which celebrity is all. Two-finger pantomimes of "attitude" and the hackneyed use of "shocking" or unsavoury materials only confirm an inability to conceive art as anything more than a means of attracting personal attention. Significantly, press coverage of a recent New York exhibition by Damien Hirst devoted far more space to breathlessly detailing the opening night's guest list than to any evaluation of the items being exhibited.

As the art world has followed a broader regression to facile infantilism, a mass-produced medium originally aimed at the juvenile now offers a rare environment in which intelligent talent has a chance to develop. Once exclusively the domain of adolescent power fantasies and vaguely homoerotic imagery, the comic book and graphic novel now harbour some of the most ambitious and articulate critiques of the surrounding cultural shrinkage. Given the improbable realities of our age, the conventions of "serious" art and literature seem suddenly mute and inadequate, too small to address the events that have overtaken them—events without precedent outside the realm of comic-book science fiction. A wider and more imaginative frame of reference is needed for a real world in which the difference between impossible and commonplace is a decade, maybe less.

Japanese *Manga* Invades America

Frederik L. Schodt

In Japan comic books are not a medium aimed exclusively at children. Millions of Japanese adults as well as young people eagerly snap up comic books on a weekly basis. Nearly everyone in Japanese society reads comics or is at least quite knowledgeable about them. Known collectively as *manga*, each of these publications is typically several hundred pages long and contains a handful of ongoing stories. *Manga* writers and artists are influenced by their American counterparts, but since their audience is more diverse, the stories range from adventure tales to historical narratives to erotic fantasies. And the writers and artists themselves are heralded as celebrities—icons of this pop-culture art form.

Manga were first imported to the United States in the late 1970s and early 1980s, but even then only a few examples broke into the market. By the late 1980s, however, American comic-book stores were flooded with *manga* titles. The drastic change was due to the surge in popularity of Japanese animated television shows and movies (called anime) that were often spin-offs of Japanese comics. As American audiences became familiar with the unique style of anime, the conventions of *manga* became less mysterious and more appealing. In the following article, interpreter, translator, and writer Frederik L. Schodt discusses *manga* mania as it captured American readers in the last two decades of the twentieth century. Since

■

Schodt's summary was written in the mid-1990s, he could only predict that *manga* would enjoy even greater commercial success in the states in the new millennium. As proven by the fact that whole sections of major bookstores are currently devoted to *manga* (not to mention the proliferation of anime television shows), it is clear that Schodt's prediction has come true. Much of the country is now cognizant of the look and stylization of Japanese comics and cartoons, even if not every American has sat down to read *manga* or watch an anime television program.

PART OF THE REASON MANGA BEGAN TO ENJOY some measure of commercial success in the mid-1980s is that many American comics fans and artists were looking for something different from the superhero genre that so dominates American comics. Keiji Nakazawa's *Barefoot Gen*, which had appeared in English in 1978, helped show many Americans how a longer, expanded format of comics could be used to create a more novelistic style. Kazuo Koike and Gōseki Kojima's beautifully rendered twenty-eight-volume samurai classic, *Kozure Ōkami* ("Lone Wolf and Cub"), helped awaken artists such as Frank Miller, the 1980s American comics superstar, to the cinematic potential of the comics medium. Partly as a result of Miller's enthusiasm, an English translation of *Lone Wolf* was published in 1987 by Chicago-based First Comics. With covers by Miller, it was an instant sensation among American comics fans.

Subsequently, nearly every major American comic book publisher has at one time or another issued translated Japanese manga or at least toyed with the idea of doing so. One of the most high-profile experiments has been Marvel Comics' publication (under its Epic Comics imprint) of Katsuhiro Ōtomo's dark sci-fi thriller *Akira*, beginning in 1988. Ōtomo draws in a detailed, realistic style familiar to Americans (he is influenced by French and American art styles and was one of the first postwar Japanese manga artists to draw Japanese with smaller eyes and a more. "Asian" look). The dystopian science-fiction theme of his long-running story about a delinquent biker with apocalyptic powers in neo-Tokyo is exactly the type of material modern American readers enjoy. Sales were helped by the legitimacy Marvel's name lent to the project, by Marvel's efforts to make the Japanese work seem as "American" as possible (even colorizing the originally black-and-white artwork), and by the existence in Japan of a highly successful animated feature film version of the manga. . . .

New Publishers, New Rules

In 1995 the largest publishers of translated manga in America were not the big East Coast comics publishers Marvel and DC, but Viz Communications and Dark Horse Comics, both on the West Coast. Reflecting the particularly high level of interest in manga in the region, and a once-close-but-now-often-tortured relationship, Viz and the manga production arm of Dark Horse—Studio Proteus—were both located in San Francisco, only a few miles from each other. Further down the list but rapidly growing was Antarctic Press, based in Texas. . . .

From the beginning, Viz had to struggle to adapt Japanese comics to the U.S. market. The company had to evolve a system of translation, often settling on a team approach, using a translator and a "rewriter" or editor of the translations for natural-sounding dialog. Since Japanese manga are read from right to left, pages also had to be flipped and "sound effects" (the *booms* and *pows*) had to be relettered. When interviewed in 1992, [editor-in-chief Satoru] Fujii commented on some of the problems the company initially faced when it first worked with an American publisher before going independent: "We had a lot of disputes over editorial policy," he says. "They were used to American comics, and wanted to adapt and change manga to fit those conventions. For example, they wanted 'thought balloons' (containing a character's thoughts, as opposed to 'speech') to always be bubble-shaped. Also, in manga 'sound effects' are an integral part of the whole drawing, but they wanted more traditional American effects."

And then there was the issue of colorization. Most American comics are in color, whereas most manga are not. This can be a major disadvantage in the mainstream U.S. marketplace. Coloring manga can be successfully done, as was the case with Marvel's version of *Akira*, but manga are designed in black and white to exploit subtle monochrome nuances and shadings, and these can be ruined by an overlay of color. Like the colorization of old black-and-white movies, colorization of manga is highly controversial. After a year or two of trying to colorize its translated manga, Viz gave up. "Some people like color," Fujii noted in 1992, "and some don't. We've found that color alone doesn't sell a manga, so we're going back to black and white.". . .

The second biggest source of translated manga in the United States in 1905 was Studio Proteus, a "manga packaging" company run by Toren Smith in San Francisco. Studio Proteus has close ties to Dark Horse, one of the largest independent comics publishers (i.e., not part of the Marvel-DC oligarchy). . . .

One characteristic of many Studio Proteus manga is that [U.S. packager of Japanese comics Toren] Smith concentrates heavily on locating works by Japanese artists who draw in a rather non-Japanese style. This, combined with Smith's talent for writing the uniquely snappy dialogue preferred by American readers, has helped the firm's survival. In addition to Katsuhiro Ōtomo's *Domu* (arguably one of the finest Japanese manga rendered into English), Studio Proteus has produced many stories by Masamune Shirow, a brilliant artist with an opaque and mysterious style of storytelling who, thanks to Studio Proteus, may have achieved cult status among U.S. fans before he did in Japan. The Shirow works issued by Studio Proteus and Dark Horse include *Dominion*, *Orion*, *Ghost in the Shell*, and the well-received *Appleseed*. . . .

The Anime Connection

As the anime industry began to explode into the North American mainstream in the mid-nineties, acquiring an increasingly hip aura on MTV and among Generation Xers, manga publishing became as linked to anime as it is in Japan, if not more so. Companies that had been issuing translated manga, such as Viz, began issuing "English-ized" anime videos directly tied in to the manga. Firms like Central Park Media, primarily an anime video importer/localizer firm, also branched out into publishing, issuing manga titles of their video releases under the logo CPM Comics. In England, the giant Manga Entertainment began English-izing anime, distributing translated manga, and even participating in the financing of the production of anime in Japan. In 1995, in an industry first, the animated theatrical feature *Ghost in the Shell*, based on Masamune Shirow's manga and jointly financed by Manga Entertainment and a Japanese production company, was simultaneously released in English and Japanese versions for mainstream distribution networks in both markets. . . .

Manga Subject Matter

The vast majority of translated manga material in America remains skewed to the idiosyncrasies of the marketplace, which is still overwhelmingly dominated by young males. Science fiction stories, with their more universal themes, are popular, and so are stories with an erotic theme. There is also a great deal of pressure on publishers to issue manga with an animation tie-in. Thus, there are lots of panty-clad girls with guns, monsters, cyber-robots, and apocalyptic visions. But if one searches, there is much more. Viz Communications issues women's manga. Blast Books in New York has published a volume of the decadent avant-garde work of Suehiro Maruo. . . . Texas-based Antarctic Press and other firms have issued several *dojinshi*, or Japanese manga fanzines, as well as a wide variety of the ever-popular Japanese erotic manga.

One of the biggest problems for readers of translated manga is that it is often difficult to find stories that have been published in their entirety. Smaller comics publishers in America, outside of the Marvel-DC orbit, have always led a precarious existence, so if they undertake to translate and publish a lengthy Japanese manga, which may be thousands of pages long, they may well not be around to complete the work. A manga story 2,000 pages long in Japan may be serialized in a weekly magazine and be finished in a little over a year. In the United States, where all "comic books" are monthlies, the same story would take nearly five years. . . .

Manga Made in America

In the English-speaking world, manga are not only read, but—increasingly—emulated. Fred Patten, in an article titled "1977–1992: Fifteen Years of North American Fandom," notes one of the first "brash" examples of Japanese anime/manga influences on an American comic book: in 1983, a character in issue 79 of Marvel Comics' *Star Wars* (scripted and drawn by Tom Palmer and manga fan Jo Duffy) was drawn as a pastiche of Leiji Matsumoto's famous Captain Harlock space-pirate character.

Today, the manga influence on American comics is far more obvious. Although American artists generally have far fewer pages to work with than their Japanese counterparts, American page layouts have become much more cinematic and dramatic and are now quite similar to those of Japanese male manga (the distinctively different layouts of women's manga make them much more difficult to emulate). In 1992, Toren Smith claimed that "the Japanese use of screen tone (for shading) is influencing American artists. Some, such as Adam Hughes, are very interested in working in black and white now because they want to try new toning techniques. . . . I've also noticed that American artists seem to be using more Japanese-style sound effects." Other Americans, such as Art Spiegelman, Pulitzer Prize–winning author of the *Maus* graphic novel series (which was very Japanese in its treatment of a serious subject in a long, narrative manga format), have even claimed that the "eyes" of characters in American comics seem to be getting larger and larger because of the Japanese influence.

So-called American manga—comic books authored by Americans but executed in a Japanese-style—are the most striking example of the manga influence on American comics. Page layouts are more dramatic and fluid, and characters have larger eyes, less muscular physiques, and rounder faces. Stories have many more allusions to Japanese culture and may feature Japanese characters or Japanese subject matter. As one might expect, the artists and writers are enormous fans of manga or anime. Some of the best-known examples in the early 1990s were Ben Dunn's popular parody *Ninja High School* and Adam Warren and Toren Smith's *Dirty Pair.* . . .

Ultimately, in the United States and other countries manga may have had their biggest effect on the publishing system itself. Just as artists have begun to emulate the Japanese style of art, publishers have tried imitating the Japanese system of doing business. Links with animation and movies are being strengthened, as are the rights of creators. Increasingly, thin American-style "comic books" are compiled into paperback book collections and sold through non-traditional channels such as trade book distributors, which gets them into regular bookstores. In an article in the April 1996 edition of *Wizard* magazine, titled "American Manga," writer Carl Gustav Horn even speculated that the growing popularity of Japanese manga might create a renaissance in the otherwise ailing U.S. comics industry. . . .

Predictions That Have Come True

In a September 17, 1995 *New York Times* article, Ty Ahmad-Taylor estimated that sales of Japanese comic books in America in the previous year amounted to $10 million and that home video sales had reached $50 million. Although many people in the industry with whom I talked seemed to feel the figure for translated manga sales was highly inflated (with the real number around $5 to $6 million), there was a general consensus that sales were growing rapidly, mainly because of the popularity of anime. Toren Smith of Studio Proteus estimates that 80 percent of his readers start out as anime fans. "A rising tide lifts all boats," he says. "Anime are becoming part of the American entertainment mainstream, and manga are becoming part of that, too."

Nonetheless, the total share of translated manga in the overall comics market remains small. In 1992, when I asked Satoru Fujii of Viz why he thought young Americans liked Japanese manga, he was quite blunt. "Most don't," he said. "To 90 percent of comics fans, manga are a foreign medium, with different artwork, different sequences, and different stories. But those who like them, *really* like them." Three years later, in 1995, he was still cautious about the future. He saw the growth of translated manga as slow, but noted that if anime truly became mainstream in the U.S. there could be quite a large fan base in ten years, when many of the small children raised on anime would begin buying manga. "If we have a large fan base," he noted hopefully, "we can start publishing the really great Japanese comics, which don't have a market now."

Explaining Manga's Popularity

In Japan, anime shows are like commercials for manga, and they are still watched mainly by younger people and *otaku* [serious fans]. Unlike manga, which have permeated mainstream, adult society, anime shows are not something your average office manager spends time watching. In the English-speaking world, however, anime programs are the entry point into a new universe for fans who are often adults. Manga—with their different "vocabulary" and "grammar" and much closer connection to the Japanese "id"—are the inner chamber for initiates. Given Rudyard Kipling's famous lines about East and West never meeting, perhaps the most remarkable aspect of translated manga is that they are popular at all. Especially interesting in America, in light of Kipling's opinion, is that there is no "Western" French or Italian or even British comics subculture.

Ultimately, the popularity of both anime and manga outside of Japan is emblematic of something much larger—perhaps a postwar "mind-meld" among the peoples of industrialized nations, who all inhabit a similar (but steadily shrinking) physical world of cars, computers, buildings, and other manmade objects and systems. Patterns of thinking are still different among cultures, and different enough for people to be fascinated by each other, but the areas of commonality have increased to the point where it is easier than ever before to reach out and understand each other on the deepest levels of human experience and emotion.

What's Wrong with Comics Today?

Gregory Cwiklik

While modern comic books have tackled more mature themes, and whole series, such as DC's Vertigo line, have been targeted at sophisticated readers, Gregory Cwiklik argues that mainstream comics today have still not grown up. In the following selection, Cwiklik insists that most comics—especially superhero comics—are poorly written and devoid of imaginative plots or artwork. Instead, he argues that most mainstream comics are filled with images of scantily clad females and violent fight scenes—two hallmarks of adolescent male fantasy. The blame for this depressing state of comics, Cwiklik maintains, belongs to both the readership and the publishers. For their part, most comics readers are more interested in collecting comics than in reading them, and those who do pore through the books seem content with little plot and the visual assault of salacious images. Catering to these lowered expectations, comics artists and writers lack enthusiasm and concentrate on churning out product. The result is splashy images covering up a lack of thoughtful plot and fully realized characters. Gregory Cwiklik is an artist and writer who frequently contributes to the *Comics Journal*, a magazine devoted to analyzing comic books and comic strips.

■

Gregory Cwiklik, "What's Wrong with Comics Today?" *The Comics Journal*, Winter 2002, pp. 37–43. Copyright © 2002 by Fantagraphics Books. Reproduced by permission.

THERE IS NOTHING INHERENTLY BAD ABOUT superheroes nor even with escapism, however one defines that term. The mystery writer Raymond Chandler once described it rather broadly as any reading done for pleasure and to lift one from the deadly tedium of everyday life. What is depressing and somewhat puzzling, however, is the inability of mainstream comics publishers and creators, with few exceptions, to deliver even worthwhile escapist entertainment. Most of the titles on display are completely lacking in imagination, intelligence or wit—on either the verbal or visual level.

Adolescent Fantasy

The biggest stumbling block to creativity seems to be the way in which mainstream comics have evolved into a closed-off, insular world geared totally to an adolescent and almost exclusively male universe of collectors and fans whose tastes revolve around superheroes, wrestling, violent animation and video games and action films. It is claimed that the average age of the typical comic-book reader is actually inching upward every year and that the average fan is in his early 20s, but the only real evidence for any age spike is the fact that many comics have become as salacious as they were in the early '50s just before the then-new Comics Code Authority clamped down. Comic-book creators have always been good at shamelessly appropriating ideas and imagery from movies. These days, the movies that really get comics artists' juices flowing are action films with an apocalyptic/supernatural/horror edge or that deal with ritualistic serial killers. So, in today's Gothic-flavored comics, superheroes do battle with the dark dominions in stories filled with demon seeds, vampire goddesses, witches, sorcerers, etcetera. There are even sword-swinging nuns (!?!) like Magdalena and Arealla who defend the Vatican. Since comics' readership is predominantly male and the companies servicing their needs [are] after their immediate financial attention and little else, the warrior women in these titles represent not so much feminist empowerment but an excuse for sexual titillation. Lady Death, who defies Heaven and Hell, wears only the tiniest ebon bikini (with matching garters and leggings) to contain her impossibly voluptuous ivory form and when Darkchylde isn't being a monster, as the artist desires. Although these sexy wonder women may be skimpily clad or even naked at times, their nipples and pubic areas are always obscured by a wisp of mist, a torn strand of cloth, or even metallic pasties. Thus these comics manage the improbable trick of being both salacious and puritanical at the same time. What's objectionable is actually not the sexiness of the strips (no pun intended) but their absurd fig-leaf prudery—which is the result of the publishers wanting to have their cake and eat it too. You see, they're in a bit of a dilemma; they're trying to sell to younger fans whose parents might object to junior getting off on pin-up material amongst the wholesome mayhem, yet at the same time publishers are trying to appeal to older, perpetually tumescent adolescent readers.

Male anatomy in comics is also exaggerated but not necessarily sexualized. These supermen may be masses of veiny, rock-like musculature but curiously, they've nothing between their legs, so they come off as iron-pumping *castrati*. No wonder they're always scowling and fighting.

Drawn-Out Plots

The insular fan-oriented nature of mainstream comics has gotten so far out of hand that its writers often make no attempt to produce material that is even comprehensible to a wider audience. Increasingly, every narrative seems to be part of some mini-series or interlinking story arc reaching across multiple titles and issues. Continuing storylines designed to keep an audience hooked are perhaps derived from current TV shows, but one can tune into an episode of *NYPD Blue* and be up to speed in a few minutes; with most of these comics the uninitiated reader is in a fog throughout. The situation is so ridiculous that even purchasing a comic labeled as issue #1 is no guarantee of getting in at the beginning. For example, issue #1 of *Witchblade/Darkness* has the marker "2 of 4" running incongruously across the bottom of the cover. The story is continued in *Darkness/Witchblade* #1. Got that? In any case, this plethora of issue #1s is merely a transparent industry scam to try to sell supposedly valuable "collector's items" to gullible buyers.

Since most comics are only about 20 pages long and with frequent splash panels and fewer panels per page, they're usually a quick read. If one is a fan of the genre, a title like *Lady*

Death provides a few imaginative touches in its story and art and the plotline is better than that of comparable movies, but the story arc just goes on forever and of course is ladled out in brief 20-page installments, so it's not very satisfying.

Churning Out Product

The lack of originality and flair in comics is not really too surprising when one looks at the attitude of the publishers. Marvel Comics is an obvious example. In current business literature the importance of brand names or *branding* takes on an almost mystical significance. Biz lit extols the success of CEOs like Disney's Michael Eisner who has parlayed the Disney name and its beloved trademarked characters into a merchandising/entertainment steamroller. Marvel has decided that its strength lies in the ownership of its own brands; i.e., the Marvel name, its trademarked characters, even (incredibly) the "Stan Lee presents" logo. It has pegged its readers as juvenile and has no interest in pursuing an adult audience except for collectors (of course) and baby-boomer parents whose fond nostalgic memories of Marvel will persuade them to take the family to theme parks featuring Spider-Man simulacrum clobbering baddies. With merchandising so important, Marvel has been irredeemably hostile to the idea of creators' rights. Hired talent cranks out "quality" product according to a successful recipe. When the recipe needs adjusting, they bring in a certified story manager, a hot name like Warren Ellis, who is contracted to write, say, three *Generation X* stories which will inject new attitude into the series. He will then stay on in a consulting capacity to manage a team of writers working from his ideas and outlines. Given its sausage-making approach to producing comics, the mediocrity of once mighty Marvel is not at all surprising.

Needless to say, the notion of a single individual or writer-artist team with a proprietary interest and control of their own creation and who exclusively write and draw each episode, putting their individual stamp on their character is anathema to companies like Marvel. Although Image Comics was formed by creators who broke away from Marvel at the height of their popularity so they could write and draw and legally own their own titles, most of these creators now have their own crews turning out the adventures of their characters on a work-for-hire basis.

DC has played a much smarter game than traditional rival Marvel. Several years ago, DC launched its Vertigo line, aimed at a more mature audience including, it was hoped, those elusive female fans. With an eye on the phenomenal success of Stephen King and other writers of weird fiction, Vertigo's emphasis has been on the supernatural—although never exclusively so—in titles such as *Sandman, Preacher, The Invisibles,* etcetera. Printed in a variety of formats and spearheaded by a slew of British writers, Vertigo has been producing comics that are actually being bought to be read, rather than for their alleged collectible status. So they deserve credit for that alone. . . .

The Vertigo titles are generally much better-written than those of their costumed brethren: they're often funnier and more biting. Many would even qualify as good escapist fiction if the artwork wasn't so consistently pedestrian. Although a certain amount of sex (mainly via verbal banter) is presented, in tone the Vertigo books are not very lascivious and women aren't portrayed as pin-up dollies. Thematically, they deal with adult subjects like religion daringly, but they're not really *adult* in the same sense as the better alternatives because they tend to avoid dealing with real-life situations. For one thing the stories invariably revolve around people with bizarre powers having supernatural adventures—that in and of itself doesn't disqualify them—what does, in my book, is their easy adherence to the artificial and overly formulaic plotlines and characterizations of popular fiction and film. They just don't delve deeply enough into the issues they bring up and I can't imagine any Vertigo creator displaying the same sort of soul-baring honesty as Justin Green or R. Crumb or Julie Doucet.

Overblown Splashiness

Artwise, the initial impression most mainstream comics make is one of slick, overblown splashiness, an effect greatly enhanced by the new use of computer coloring. At one end of the stylistic spectrum is what might be called the Image look [referring to the artistic style of the Image Comics company] which dominated the field a few years ago and which still holds sway in many quarters. In these comics the heroic icon of the superhero dominates all: Like an El Greco figure on steroids, the Image superman is wildly attenuated and bulging with massive knots of corded muscle; the superwoman is all long legs and monster boobs. At its best, a vibrant, slashing style of cross-hatching gives a dramatic sheen to the drawing. The hyper-exaggerated anatomy is mixed with the dizzying action and dramatic page layouts of Japanese comics and studded with big multiple-page splash panels. In some comics, distortion of form and musculature have been pushed into the realm of the freakish. The Hulk (and others of his ilk) is depicted as a monstrous screeching mass of muscle with an absurdly tiny microcephalic head. In many books, elongation of the figure is so severe that it looks as though the drawings have been stretched on a piece of silly putty. An air of breathless, hyperbolic excess dominates comics pictorial storytelling, too: It's like the visual equivalent of listening to a not very good play in which every line is delivered in a shout. If visuals can be said to exude stupidity, these comics scream it. At the other end of the spectrum lies a less ornate style of work used primarily for the non-costumed heroes. Here layouts are less splashy and anatomical excess is far less overt. But by far the overwhelming majority of comic book artwork falls into that vast middle ground between where a simplified version of the Image look prevails.

Generally speaking, the skill level in these books runs the gamut, but what's most depressing is the utter sameness of it all. Formula repeats itself in one comic after another. So lacking in originality or individuality is the bulk of the work being done that one might be forgiven for thinking that only a handful of different artists working in a few closely related styles were turning out the entire comics industry output. These visual clichés are even codified in "how to" books published by the industry.

While some of the artists are just bad, others are probably better than the material allows. One example: Liam McCormack-Sharp's artwork on *Spawn: The Dark Ages* is a bit rough and sloppy in places but elsewhere it's obvious he is a skilled craftsman who knows how to render form and at his best his linework flows with a Celtic sinuousness. The difficulty arises from having a "medieval" tale adapted to the conventions of the superhero comic that are deemed requisite to please an Image Comics audience. So the main character is a super-exaggerated muscleman with ridiculous spiked shoulderpads and a head/helmet with oversized grinning teeth. Plus Sharp's depictions of women often fly in the face of the latest archaeological evidence that clearly shows that neither silicone implants nor Nautilus fitness machines were available at the time of the Crusades. So comic art with some potential is marred by its adherence to standard comics drivelry.

It's not as though simplicity of line, high exaggeration or even gross cartooniness are bad in themselves, but they need to be applied with some skill and intelligence. To a certain extent various elements conspire to retard comic books. The labor required to knock out the multiplicity of images that comic strip production requires day in and day out is both intensive and repetitive. It discourages working from life and encourages formulization, shortcuts, and cliché. In many books the sexy main characters may be rendered with a certain élan while the rest of the art is sloughed off. Understandably, deadline pressures make dependability a far greater asset to publishers than mere talent. There are exceptions to the general run of mediocrity; Mike Mignola, Paul Pope, Brian Bolland, Glenn Fabry, Mike Kaluta, Mark Schultz, Dave Stevens, Charles Vess and a few others come to mind, but a number of these seem to be primarily employed to provide attractive covers while leaving the mass-produced interior hackwork to others, thereby continuing a tradition of deceptive packaging that dates back to the dawn of comic book publishing.

Bad, simplistic artwork is often covered up to some degree by the use of newer, more sophisticated printing methods, especially computer coloring which gives comics deeper colors and added tonal range. A good example can be seen in a sequence from a recent episode of a *Darkchylde* in which monsters battle in a moonlit woods. The actual drawing is pedestrian at best, but the rich color effects—deep acid-greens and blues with warm, glowing highlights—combine to give the pages an overheated expressionistic jungle look. Unfortunately, this coloring process is usually overdone and even some of the better books suffer from a gleaming, robotic lack of humanity. . . .

Missed Opportunities

There have been attempts by the mainline axis to think "outside the box" but they haven't often fared well. A good example of this is the earnest, oversize volume *Superman: Peace on Earth*. The painted art of Alex Ross has a startling effect as hitherto flat pen-and-ink superheroes come to life as fully-visualized characters, but this volume shares the same difficulty as his earlier Marvels in that the more realistic the art and situations, the more incongruous the presence of the superhero, especially an all-powerful one like Superman. Here Superman, who has been flitting from one disaster to another, decides to get serious about world hunger and mobilize global will to stamp it out. But when he tries to deliver boxcars of food, smiling dictators try to commandeer or destroy these goods in the name of national sovereignty. The obvious problem here is that the difficulties faced by real people giving aid are not those that should confound an omnipotent Man of Steel. At one point, he laments the tragedies that have befallen a crowd of Bosnians, but that begs the question of what Superman was doing all the time said Bosnians were being slaughtered. Couldn't he have liberated the concentration camps or silenced the guns around Sarajevo or brought modern war criminals to justice at The Hague? Why does Superman melt the rifles of a corrupt dictator's troops instead of the dictator's head? Even if the writer has decided that Superman is too much of a goody-two-shoes to act extra-legally, that needs to be the focus. There just isn't room in the real world for a Superman. The only truly interesting sort of work would have been a far more imaginative scenario along the lines of a "King Superman"-type story in which the Man of Steel decides to set things straight. Otherwise the premise just doesn't make sense. A story in which Superman concludes that people have just got to start loving one another is just not going to do it.

Kyle Baker's graphic novels are much like Hollywood romantic comedies. The dialogue and interplay between characters is smart and clever but in both *Why I Hate Saturn* and *You Are Here* the humorous banter and situations turn incongruously ugly and violent. In dramatic terms, I don't think either piece really manages to reconcile the drastic change in tone.

Baker does draw beautifully, however, and *You Are Here* is reminiscent of an amazing super Technicolor cartoon from the '50s or '60s—stylized, splashy and lush with vivid purple, red, and green hues.

Ted Nomura's *World War II, 1946* is part of the Altered Histories series that imagines what would've happened if historical events had gone differently. Strangely, the plot of *WW II, 1946: Born To Die* (a young Japanese man who wants to draw comics but who instead dies as a Kamikaze pilot) in no way requires an altered past, so the premise is wasted. The manga-style [referring to Japanese comics] figures are also pretty crude. Plus, Nomura tries to soft-soap Japan's aggressive actions and widespread atrocities with a sappy "war is terrible" gloss even though Japan's conquests of its neighbors were no more "defensive" than Hitler's invasion of Poland. What would have been illuminating would have been letting the reader see the situation through the eyes of one of the xenophobic, ultra-nationalist military caste who formed Japanese policy—to get inside the psyche of an individual operating from a radically different system of values than the reader's. The opportunity to use the freedom of fiction and the pictorial possibilities of the comics medium to delve into fascinating, dangerous and uncharted waters has been passed up.

To a large degree the same basic criticism can be leveled toward Frank Miller's *300*, which recounts the last stand of the Spartans at Thermopylae in the 5th century b.c. Art-wise, Miller is much better, of course, but although Miller did considerable historical research on the subject, he seems to have purposely glossed over certain aspects of Spartan society that he felt would have "turned off" readers (according to his *Journal* interview), such as Sparta's economy being based on slavery. But slave labor was crucial, not incidental, to maintaining the Spartan military machine that Miller admires. Once again, the trick would have been to portray the Spartan warrior as he was and still make one perceive the heroism in his actions.

To sum up bluntly, what's wrong with mainstream comics is that—with few exceptions—they too-perfectly reflect the limited worldview of a juvenile audience whose tastes and sensibilities have been shaped and circumscribed by a moronic popular culture. That many of these juveniles are in their 20s or older is no matter. They are the core constituency; the only group that can be counted upon to buy comic books on a regular basis. One can't help but conclude that the worldview and aesthetic concerns of mainstream comic-book creators are likewise limited. If mainstream creators stay in the superhero/fantasy box, it's because they like it there. They are usually fans of genre material; receiving pay to work in the field is a dream come true. With few exceptions, individuals with a more sophisticated view modify their work to fit within genre parameters.

FOR FURTHER RESEARCH

Books

Michael Barrier and Martin Williams, eds., *A Smithsonian Book of Comic-Book Comics*. New York: Smithsonian Institution Press, 1981.
> This collection is not a critical work. It has little text, but the book's value is in duplicating full-length stories from classic comic books.

Mike Benton, *The Comic Book in America: An Illustrated History*. Dallas: Taylor, 1989.
> Benton provides a chronological progress of comics from the 1930s to the 1980s. He also includes a look at genres of comics as well as a useful section that lists all the major comics publishers.

Mila Bongco, *Reading Comics: Language, Culture, and the Concept of the Superhero in Comic Books*. New York: Garland, 2000.
> Part of a series in popular culture studies, Bongco's work offers critical essays on reading comics, conventions of superhero comics, and the place of comics in pop culture. The text is scholarly but illuminating for those who want a serious look at an art form that is commonly believed to be kid stuff.

David Carrier, *The Aesthetics of Comics*. University Park: Pennsylvania State University Press, 2000.
> In this work, Carrier studies the visual elements of comic strips, comic books, and political cartoons. His references to specific artistic theories and theorists may be daunting to some readers, but his analysis is revealing, forcing his audience to recognize that "reading" comics is a unique form of literacy.

Ian Gordon, *Comic Strips and Consumer Culture, 1890–1945*. Washington, DC: Smithsonian Institution Press, 1998.
> This is a fascinating study that examines how comic-strip and comic-book stories have worked to reinforce consumer culture in America, while at the same time the comics industry has sought to take advantage of that same buying power.

Gary Groth and Robert Fiore, eds., *The New Comics*. Berkeley, CA: Berkley Books, 1988.

Capitalizing on the then-recent trend toward more adult-oriented comics, the editors collected interviews with such diverse artists as Frank Miller, Robert Crumb, and Kim Deitch. The interviews were culled from the pages of *The Comics Journal* and give some insider views of the industry and changing attitudes toward comics.

Maurice Horn, *Comics of the American West*. New York: Winchester Press, 1977.

This is the definitive exploration of Western comic art. Horn details cowboy series as well as non-Western comics that dabbled with Western themes and characters.

M. Thomas Inge, *Comics as Culture*. Jackson: University Press of Mississippi, 1990.

This is a well-respected volume on the cultural impact of comic strips and comic books on America. Inge explores how comics images and speech have been appropriated by pop art, advertising, literature, and even common slang.

Dick Lupoff and Don Thompson, eds., *All in Color for a Dime*. New York: Ace Books, 1970.

This anthology is an interesting collection of nostalgic reminiscences of comic books' Golden and Silver Ages. The focus is on how comics helped shaped the lives and experiences of the individual authors of these essays, yet the writers—many of whom are familiar names in the field—do much to generalize their experiences to exemplify the greater cultural significance of comics.

Scott McCloud, *Understanding Comics: The Invisible Art*. New York: HarperCollins, 1993.

This now-seminal examination of comics is told entirely in comic-book format. The postmodern trick of using the medium to explain the medium works exceedingly well, as McCloud is able to literally illustrate the inner workings and strategies of comic books as he defines them.

Amy Kiste Nyberg, *Seal of Approval: The History of the Comics Code*. Jackson: University Press of Mississippi, 1998.

Nyberg gives a detailed account of the crusade against comics in the 1950s and the subsequent Comics Code that the industry adopted to quell public fears that comics were corrupting America's youth.

Matthew Pustz, *Comic Book Culture: Fanboys and True Believers.* Jackson: University Press of Mississippi, 1999.

Pustz maintains that comic-book creators and their fans have done much to fashion an entire subculture devoted to the medium. Entire communities exist within the letters pages of comic books, comic-book shops, comics conventions, and Web sites that show how diverse and widespread the power of the comic book is in America.

Jordan Raphael and Tom Spurgeon, *Stan Lee and the Rise and Fall of the American Comic Book.* Chicago: Chicago Review Press, 2003.

This thorough biography of the man who created many of Marvel Comics' most memorable characters gives insight not only into Lee's creative process but also the operation of a major comics publisher.

Maria Reidelbach, *Completely MAD: A History of the Comic Book and Magazine.* Boston: Little, Brown, 1991.

Using many illustrations taken from *MAD*, Reidelbach traces the history of the satirical, antiestablishment comic magazine that garnered a huge following. Also included in the pages of Reidelbach's book are many interviews with the odd cast of characters who made *MAD* a humor institution.

Reinhold Reitberger and Wolfgang Fuchs, *Comics: Anatomy of a Mass Medium.* Boston: Little, Brown, 1971.

Written by two Germans with a passion for comics and media culture, this work has been a touchstone of comics criticism for three decades. The authors examine nearly every facet of comics and comic culture (through 1970) in a deceptively brief amount of space. Sadly, the book contains many errors that escaped correction.

Richard Reynolds, *Super Heroes: A Modern Mythology.* Jackson: University Press of Mississippi, 1992.

Distinguishing superheroes from other heroes in legend and reality, Reynolds examines the common traits and story lines of comic books.

Trina Robbins, *From Girls to Grrrlz: A History of Women's Comics from Teens to Zines.* San Francisco: Chronicle Books, 1999.

Trina Robbins is an artist who came out of the underground comix movement in the 1960s to begin fashioning her own female-oriented comix in the 1970s. With invaluable insider knowledge,

Robbins examines the evolution of women in comics—both as the subject matter of comic books and as comics artists.

Patrick Rosenkranz, *Rebel Visions: The Underground Comix Revolution, 1963–1975*. Seattle: Fantagraphics, 2002.
An exhaustive overview of the underground scene, Rosenkranz's narrative weaves together the remembrances of the artists who wrote and drew these unique comics. The book is profusely illustrated and contains many short biographies of the major artists.

William W. Savage Jr., *Commies, Cowboys, and Jungle Queens: Comic Books and America, 1945–1954*. Hanover, NH: Wesleyan University Press, 1990.
Another key text in comics criticism, Savage's book illustrates how specific Cold War cultural events (such as the Korean War and the proliferation of the atom bomb) shaped and were reflected in comic books of the time.

Bradford W. Wright, *Comic Book Nation: The Transformation of Youth Culture in America*. Baltimore: Johns Hopkins University Press, 2001.
A critical examination of the power of comic books upon various generations of America's youth. Wright focuses on the historical context that shapes comic books—examining the influence of producers as well as consumers on the medium. According to Wright, adolescence is both a market to be exploited and a "cultural obsession" in America. Comics are, thus, a perfect example of the two trends impinging on the nation's youth.

Nicky Wright, *The Classic Era of American Comics*. Lincolnwood, IL: Contemporary Comics, 2000.
Wright divides the comic books of the 1930s through 1950s into thematic categories such as horror, Western, and girls' comics. In each section, the author meticulously documents the history and any related controversies of the comic book's Golden Age.

Internet Resources

Comic Book Resources, www.comicbookresources.com
This Web site is devoted mainly to fans. It has some reviews and commentary and can get the uninitiated up-to-speed on the current state of comics publication. The site also has its own elec-

tronic publication, but the stories are limited mostly to comics events and new story lines.

Image & Narrative, www.imageandnarrative.be/index.htm

Image & Narrative is an online journal of the visual arts. While not limited to comic books, the site's archive has many excellent essays on the visual style and narrative workings of comics.

Sir Real's Underground Comix Classix, http://sir.real.50megs. com/comix/

Visitors can view the covers of many comix from the 1960s and 1970s. This is a collector's site, and although not very extensive, it is one of the few on the Internet devoted to this topic.

INDEX

DATE DUE